6512

DATE DUE

SEP 2 2 1992			
OCT 2 2 199			
0 2 1992			
FEB 0 3 1993			
APR 0 1998			

AMERICA The BEAUTIFUL

TENNESSEE

By Sylvia McNair

Consultants

Bruce Opie, Social Studies Consultant, Tennessee Department of Education

Charles W. Crawford, Ph.D., Director, Oral History Research Office, Memphis State University

Herbert L. Harper, Executive Director, Tennessee Historical Commission

Robert L. Hillerich, Ph.D., Bowling Green State University, Bowling Green, Ohio

CHILDRENS PRESS®
CHICAGO

A night view of Gatlinburg, in the Great Smoky Mountains

Project Editor: Joan Downing
Associate Editor: Shari Joffe
Design Director: Margrit Fiddle
Typesetting: Graphic Connections, Inc.
Engraving: Liberty Photoengraving

Library of Congress Cataloging-in-Publication Data

McNair, Sylvia.
  America the beautiful. Tennessee / by Sylvia
McNair.
     p.   cm.
  Includes index.
  Summary: Introduces the geography, history,
government, economy, industry, culture, historic
sites, and famous people of the Volunteer State.
   ISBN 0-516-00488-3
  1. Tennessee—Juvenile literature.
[1. Tennessee.] I. Title.
F436.3.M36 1990   89-25285
976.8—dc20   CIP
                                    AC

Visitors enjoy the twice-daily Parade of the Ducks at the Peabody Hotel in Memphis. These ducks march over a red carpet to the accompaniment of band music and spend their days in the hotel's lobby fountain.

TABLE OF CONTENTS

Chapter 1

THE THREE STATES OF TENNESSEE

THE THREE STATES OF TENNESSEE

At one time, billboards near the state's borders read Welcome to the Three States of Tennessee. That is how Tennesseans think of their state. These three states of Tennessee—East, Middle, and West—have marked differences in politics, industry, agriculture, and culture. All these differences stem from Tennessee's geography and how it has shaped the way the people have lived.

One way in which the land has affected life in the three states of Tennessee is shown in the style of music that has evolved in each section. When the first westward-moving pioneers found their way through the mountain passes of the Appalachians and down into the river valleys of Tennessee, they brought their music with them: the folk songs of England, Scotland, and Ireland. Over the years, through the isolation of mountain living, the mountain music of East Tennessee evolved.

When slaves were brought to the cotton fields of West Tennessee's Mississippi bottomlands, they lightened the burden of their work by singing. These work songs became another kind of Tennessee music—the blues—that was later made popular by musicians such as the renowned Memphis musician-composer W. C. Handy. Today's rock and roll, a descendant of the blues, was first recorded in Memphis.

Nashville, in the level land of Middle Tennessee, is the country music capital of the world. Country music is a blend of the folk songs and ballads of Appalachia and the blues of the bottomlands.

All the styles of Tennessee's music are popular far beyond the state's borders. Just to think of Tennessee brings a smile to the face of those who know its three states.

Chapter 2
THE LAND

THE LAND

On a map of the United States, Tennessee is easy to identify by its shape. It is roughly a parallelogram with nearly straight lines across its long borders on the north and south and jagged ones on the east and west. It is about four times as long from east to west (430 miles/692 kilometers) as it is from north to south (110 miles/ 177 kilometers).

Tennessee, with an area of 42,114 square miles (109,075 square kilometers), shares its borders with eight states: North Carolina to the east; Virginia and Kentucky to the north; Missouri and Arkansas to the west across the Mississippi River; and Mississippi, Alabama, and Georgia to the south. Of all the fifty states, only Missouri borders on as many states.

AN AERIAL VIEW

Imagine that you are in an airplane, flying across the state of Tennessee from the Mississippi River. It's a clear day, and you are headed due east toward Asheville, North Carolina. You are about to see Tennessee's six land regions: the East Gulf Coastal Plain, the Highland Rim, the Nashville Basin, the Cumberland Plateau, the Appalachian Ridge and Valley, and the Blue Ridge. Then you will understand why Tennessee is thought of as three almost separate states.

First you're flying over plains that rise gradually from steep bluffs along the Mississippi River to a hilly strip of land on the west side of the Tennessee River. The Tennessee is a wide and

Fall Creek Falls State Park, in the Cumberland Plateau region

mighty river here. Great dams have tamed its flow and turned it into a series of lakes. This is West Tennessee.

East of the Tennessee River is a hilly region called the Highland Rim, which surrounds the Nashville Basin. Middle Tennessee is like a deep, oval serving dish (the Nashville Basin) with a broad rim (the Highland Rim). As you fly east beyond Nashville, you begin to see hills again, the eastern side of the Highland Rim. All this is Middle Tennessee.

Then, suddenly, there's an abrupt rise in the land, almost like a long wall that stretches as far as you can see. At the top of the wall you see a broad, flat region. This is the Cumberland Plateau, the beginning of East Tennessee.

Once again, you glimpse a great river that widens into artificially made lakes. It's the Tennessee River again, which starts just east of Knoxville in East Tennessee, winds down into northern Alabama and Mississippi, and turns northward again through western Tennessee and Kentucky on its way to join the Ohio River.

Now you see more mountain ridges, higher and broader than the hills of the Highland Rim. This is the Appalachian Ridge and Valley. Ridge after ridge is lined up in an orderly pattern, all running diagonally from northeast to southwest. Higher and higher they go. A bluish-grey haze appears, and there in the distance you see some real giants, topped with snow. Those are the Great Smoky Mountains, and they mark the Tennessee-North Carolina border in the Blue Ridge region. Let's land our airplane now and take a closer look at the land of Tennessee.

WEST TENNESSEE

The land region in West Tennessee is a part of the East Gulf Coastal Plain, a flat, fertile strip of land that stretches from the southern tip of Illinois to the Gulf of Mexico. A narrow strip along the Mississippi River itself is called the Mississippi Alluvial Plain. The word *alluvial* refers to the deposits of silt, clay, and gravel washed onto the land by the action of the river.

West Tennessee is primarily agricultural land with many small towns. Memphis is its only large city. Cotton, soybeans, and timber are the main agricultural products of West Tennessee. Memphis is a major center for cotton trading and hardwood manufacturing.

MIDDLE TENNESSEE

The land regions in Middle Tennessee are the Highland Rim and the Nashville Basin. The Highland Rim is a high plain,

Soybeans are one of the main agricultural products grown in West Tennessee.

formed mainly of limestone, with steep slopes that end in the Nashville Basin. Red cedar forests that cover part of the hilly Highland Rim make lumbering an important activity in this region. Mineral deposits of oil, natural gas, limestone, and iron are also found here. Beneath the surface of the Highland Rim, the activity of underground streams has hollowed out caves.

The Nashville Basin, surrounded by the Highland Rim, has some of the richest farmland in the state. Limestone, which lies beneath the surface, gives the soil the nutrients needed for growing crops and for pasturelands. Tobacco, wheat, tomatoes, potatoes, and fruit trees are just a few of the crops produced from this rich soil. Fine beef and dairy cattle, sheep, and the famous Tennessee Walking Horses are raised in Middle Tennessee.

Nashville, the state capital and the state's second-largest city, is in the middle of the basin. Clarksville, the state's fifth-largest city, is in the Highland Rim.

Fertile farmland of East Tennessee

EAST TENNESSEE

East Tennessee's land regions are the Cumberland Plateau, the Appalachian Ridge and Valley, and the Blue Ridge. The coves and valleys of the Cumberland Plateau's western edge merge with the Highland Rim. The plateau's high, wooded land has flat-topped mountains ranging from 1,500 to 1,800 feet (457 to 549 meters) high. V-shaped valleys, such as the Sequatchie Valley, cut through parts of this region.

Tennessee's fourth-largest city, Chattanooga, is located on the eastern edge of the Cumberland Plateau. Large deposits of coal, oil, and natural gas are found in this region.

East of the Cumberland Plateau is the Appalachian Ridge and Valley. An area about 55 miles (88 kilometers) wide, it alternates between sharp, wooded mountain ridges and broad, fertile

A view of Gatlinburg from a lookout in the foothills of the Smoky Mountains

valleys. Like the Nashville Basin, the Appalachian Ridge and Valley has rich soil for farming. Tobacco, wheat, and peaches are a few of the crops produced here. This region also has large deposits of limestone, sandstone, marble, zinc, and iron. Tennessee's third-largest city, Knoxville, is located here.

The Blue Ridge lies on both sides of the Tennessee-North Carolina border. Within the Blue Ridge are several mountain ranges: the Bald, Chilhowee, Great Smoky, Holston, Iron, Roan, Stone, and Unicoi mountains. Clingmans Dome, the highest peak in the state at 6,643 feet (2,025 meters), is in Great Smoky Mountains National Park. In fact, some of the highest peaks in the eastern United States are in the Blue Ridge. Much of the region's soil is too poor for farming, but large granite, copper, and iron deposits are found here.

RIVERS AND LAKES

Tennessee has three main river systems: the Mississippi, the Cumberland, and the Tennessee. The Mississippi River, which forms Tennessee's entire western boundary, drains West Tennessee. Tributaries that flow into the Mississippi River from Tennessee include the Forked Deer, Hatchie, Loosahatchie, Obion, and Wolf rivers.

With its source in Kentucky, the Cumberland River flows east to west across the northern part of Middle Tennessee before winding back to Kentucky and the Ohio River. In Tennessee, the Cumberland's tributaries are the Caney Fork, Harpeth, Red, and Stones rivers.

The Tennessee River, with its source in East Tennessee where the French Broad and Holston rivers meet, flows southwest until it enters Alabama, just southwest of Chattanooga. Entering the state again at the Alabama-Mississippi-Tennessee border, it flows north into Kentucky on its way to the Ohio River. Its entire 650-mile (1,046-kilometer) course is open to commercial navigation.

In the east, the Tennessee River's main tributaries include the Clinch, Hiwassee, Ocoee, and Little Tennessee rivers. Its main tributaries in the west include the Big Sandy, Buffalo, and Duck rivers.

Since 1933, through the work of the Tennessee Valley Authority (TVA) and the U.S. Army Corps of Engineers, a series of dams have been built along the Cumberland and Tennessee rivers in Kentucky, Tennessee, and Alabama. These dams have created artificial lakes that are known as the Great Lakes of the South. Some of the largest of these lakes in Tennessee are Kentucky, Barkley, Old Hickory, Dale Hollow, Chickamauga, Watts Bar,

Reelfoot Lake, Tennessee's largest natural lake, was formed by an earthquake.

Norris, and Douglas lakes. Reelfoot Lake, in the northwestern
corner of the state, is Tennessee's largest natural lake—but it
did not exist until 1811. Between December 16, 1811, and
March 15, 1812, a severe earthquake and its aftershocks rumbled
through the area where Missouri, Kentucky, and Tennessee meet.
Some experts say that this was the most violent earthquake ever
to hit the continental United States. It caused the Mississippi
River to change its course and with one great wave leave behind
a large lake where a forest of cottonwood, cypress, and walnut
trees had been. The lake is very shallow, and stumps and
skeletons of the huge old trees can still be seen beneath the
water.

CLIMATE

Except in the mountains, Tennessee enjoys a temperate climate most of the year. Average temperatures range from about 40 degrees Fahrenheit (4 degrees Celsius) in January to 79 degrees Fahrenheit (26 degrees Celsius) in July. The state's highest recorded temperature was 113 degrees Fahrenheit (45 degrees Celsius) at Perryville on August 9, 1930. The lowest, minus 32 degrees Fahrenheit (minus 36 degrees Celsius), was recorded at Mountain City on December 30, 1917. Spells of cold weather and snow do not usually linger very long. In East Tennessee, however, subzero weather and snow are common in winter months.

There are not many severe storms, although tornadoes occasionally touch down in West Tennessee. Average precipitation in the state is 52 inches (132 centimeters) a year.

PLANTS AND ANIMALS

Tennesseans boast that they have every type of animal and insect, and every type of tree and shrub that can be found between the Gulf of Mexico and Canada. This is an exaggeration, but at least 150 types of native trees, 81 species of mammals, and 259 species of birds reside in or migrate through the state.

Almost half of Tennessee is forested with a great variety of trees. Throughout the state, ash, beech, chestnut, elm, hickory, maple, oak, walnut, and tulip trees can be found. Flowering trees such as dogwoods, magnolias, and redbuds also grow in Tennessee. Basswood, buckeye, hemlock, spruce, and white pine trees can be found in East Tennessee's forests. Red cedars are common in Middle Tennessee, and bald cypress, cottonwood, tupelo gum, and water oak trees are native to West Tennessee.

Trout lilies and wood ducks are among the state's wild plants and birds.

Azaleas, holly, mountain laurel, and rhododendrons color the landscape of the Blue Ridge every spring. Wildflowers such as passionflowers, dragonroot, hop clover, and yellow jasmine grow throughout the state.

The vast wilderness of the Smoky Mountains provides a home for raccoons, deer, black bears, and wild boars. Skunks, beavers, muskrats, rabbits, and foxes live in fields and forests throughout the state. Tennessee's many rivers, lakes, and streams have black bass, walleyes, saugers, crappies, white bass, catfish, bluegills, bream, and trout.

Ducks, geese, quail, and wild turkeys are plentiful game birds in Tennessee. Common songbirds include robins, eastern bluebirds, cardinals, wood thrushes, and mockingbirds.

Several state agencies work to protect the state's natural environment. The Wildlife Resources Agency has a protection program for endangered and threatened species. The Department of Conservation develops state parks and forest preserves, and the Department of Health and Environment monitors water and air pollution.

Chapter 3

THE PEOPLE

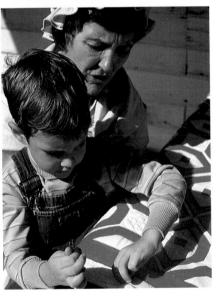

THE PEOPLE

The mountains, the valleys, and the rivers of Tennessee have
been powerful influences on its history and the character of its
people. So, too, has its location—a crossroads between North and
South and between East and West.

Only a few decades ago, many tiny settlements in the
mountains of East Tennessee were isolated, with almost no contact
with the outside world. Whole families could go through their
entire lives without ever seeing a stranger. Interstate highways
have changed that. Half the people in the United States live within
500 miles (805 kilometers) of Tennessee, and a good many of them
have visited—or at least driven through—the state.

WHO ARE THE TENNESSEANS?

Tennessee's first permanent white settlers were British colonists
from Virginia who built homes in the Watauga River Valley.
Others, many of them of Scotch-Irish origin, came from
Pennsylvania. There were also a few Germans, Welsh, Irish, and
Huguenots, but historians tell us that the Scotch-Irish were the
major influence in early Tennessee. At that time, all of the
Tennessee region was considered to be part of North Carolina.

Many of these early settlers brought black slaves into the region.
Most of them were used to work in the cotton fields of West

More than half of all Tennesseans are descended from English, Scotch-Irish, German, and Italian settlers.

Tennessee. By 1840, this group numbered 183,057 — about a quarter of the total population. At that same time, there were about 5,000 free blacks in Tennessee. After the Civil War, the black population increased for a time, as many freed slaves came into East Tennessee from Virginia and North Carolina.

TODAY'S POPULATION

The proportion of blacks has been decreasing over the past century, however, and now they make up only about 15 percent of the total population. Most of the rest of the state's population is white (83.5 percent). Well over half of these are descended from English, Scotch-Irish, German, and Italian settlers. Less than 1 percent of the population is Hispanic, and less than 0.25 percent is Native American.

The First Presbyterian Church, Kingsport

Immigration has had little impact on Tennessee recently. According to the 1980 United States census, 99 percent of Tennessee's 4,591,120 people had been born in the United States.

WHERE THEY LIVE

Until 1960, the majority of Tennessee's population lived on farms and in tiny rural settlements. By the time of the 1980 census, however, 60 percent of Tennesseans lived in towns and cities of more than 2,500. Most of these city dwellers live in the state's large cities: Memphis, Nashville, Knoxville, Chattanooga, Clarksville, Jackson, Johnson City, and Murfreesboro.

RELIGION

Tennessee is in the heart of what is popularly called the Bible Belt of America. The nickname refers to the heavy influence of fundamentalist Protestant groups, whose members believe in a literal interpretation of the Bible.

Early settlers were predominantly Baptists, Methodists, and Presbyterians. Three new churches were formed in Tennessee in the early 1800s: the Disciples of Christ, the Church of Christ, and the Cumberland Presbyterians.

Today, about 25 percent of Tennesseans belong to the Southern Baptist church. Methodists are second in number of members, followed by the Church of Christ and the Presbyterians. Roman Catholics number less than 125,000, and there are fewer than 19,000 Jews.

POLITICS

Before the Civil War, Tennessee had a vigorous two-party system. For nearly a hundred years after that conflict ended, the state was a part of the so-called Solid South. That name refers to the fact that all the former Confederate states could be counted on to vote with the Democratic party.

East Tennessee, however, most of whose residents sided with the North during the war, has been a Republican stronghold since the Civil War.

Since World War II, the results of presidential elections have swung back and forth between Republicans and Democrats. Tennessee also has elected distinguished United States senators from both parties. Tennesseans, however, have elected only two Republican governors since 1945.

Chapter 4
EARLY DAYS AND
SETTLEMENT

EARLY DAYS AND SETTLEMENT

EARLY INDIAN GROUPS

The first people known to have lived in the region of Tennessee are generally called Mound Builders. About one thousand years ago, they lived in villages along the rivers of the present states of Illinois, Indiana, Ohio, Kentucky, Georgia, Mississippi, and Tennessee.

The Mound Builders used the huge earthen mounds to support their houses and temples. In smaller, cone-shaped mounds they buried their dead, along with funeral gifts of pottery, shell spoons, and copper breastplates. These gifts were probably meant to help the deceased in the afterlife.

What is believed to be the second-largest mound in the United States is near Pinson, in southwestern Tennessee. Other important clusters of mounds are in Shiloh National Military Park, on a bluff above the Tennessee River; and at Chucalissa, in Memphis near the Mississippi River.

Long before the first European settlers arrived, the Mound Builders had disappeared. Three major groups of Native Americans then claimed areas in Tennessee: the Cherokees in the northern part of East and Middle Tennessee, the Creeks in southeastern Tennessee, and the Chickasaws in West Tennessee.

EARLY EXPLORATION

When Spanish explorers under the leadership of Hernando De Soto crossed the region in 1540-41, they raided Creek villages, passed through Cherokee land, and received gifts from the Chickasaws. More than a hundred years later, two British explorers—Gabriel Arthur and James Needham—traveled into the Tennessee River Valley.

After René-Robert Cavelier, Sieur de La Salle, claimed the Mississippi Valley for France in 1682, French settlers began to move into the region. In 1714, a French trading post was established at French Lick, near present-day Nashville, by Charles Charleville.

At that time, all three countries—Spain, France, and Great Britain—claimed ownership of Tennessee. By 1754, only France and Great Britain had claims in the region. Both British and French traders competed for the fur trade with the Indians. The Cherokees and Chickasaws were friendly with the British, and the Creeks favored the French.

In 1754, the French and Indian War broke out between the British and French and their Indian allies. When this war ended in 1763, the British gained all of France's land east of the Mississippi River. The Tennessee region became part of the colony of North Carolina.

Settlers from Pennsylvania, Virginia, and North Carolina began to cross the mountains into the Tennessee region. In 1769, William Bean and others from North Carolina formed a settlement on the Watauga River. Soon other settlements were established between the Watauga and Nolichucky rivers.

Because the little groups of log cabins were isolated and far removed from one another, these early settlers built forts for protection and established their own local governments. In 1772, the settlers formed the Watauga Association, which is recognized today as the first American attempt at complete and democratic self-government. To make and carry out laws, the settlers elected five magistrates. When the British colonial governor in North Carolina heard about it, he said the association was "a dangerous example to the people of America."

A North Carolinian by the name of Richard Henderson was interested in these territories beyond the mountains. He formed the Transylvania Land Company for the purpose of speculating in land; that is, he bought land hoping to sell it at a higher price later. Henderson employed the services of a skilled woodsman named Daniel Boone to mark trails into the unexplored territories. Boone cut a trail from Virginia through the mountains into Kentucky at the Cumberland Gap. This trail became known as the Wilderness Trail and was the main route into Tennessee.

In 1775, Henderson's company negotiated a huge real estate deal with the local Cherokees. At a place called Sycamore Shoals, they agreed to a treaty that exchanged more than 20 million acres (about 8 million hectares) in Kentucky and Tennessee for £10,000 (about $50,000) worth of goods. The Transylvania Purchase was one of the most flagrant swindles of Native Americans.

A year later, Cherokee warriors who opposed the Transylvania Purchase made a surprise attack on Fort Watauga but were not successful in destroying it. In 1777, the Cherokees met with representatives of Virginia and North Carolina to make peace. They also agreed to stay out of the war between the American colonies and Britain—the American Revolution—which had started in 1775.

In 1779, Henderson sold land on the Cumberland River to a group of settlers. They built a fort on the bank of the Cumberland

Daniel Boone (left, in center), working for the Transylvania Land Company, cut the trail that would be the main route into Tennessee from Virginia. In 1775, the same land company negotiated the Transylvania Purchase at Sycamore Shoals (right).

in 1780 and named it Fort Nashborough. These settlers drew up the Cumberland Compact for the governing of their village. In 1784, three years after the American Revolution ended, the North Carolina legislature renamed the settlement Nashville.

THE OVERMOUNTAIN MEN

Sycamore Shoals, the site of the Transylvania Purchase, was also the site of a dramatic event that helped lead to the final success of the American Revolution. By 1780, the war had been dragging on for five long years. The South was almost entirely under the control of the British commander, Lord Cornwallis. However, up in the mountains of Tennessee, North Carolina, and Virginia were frontier settlements that had not been brought into submission by British forces. In fact, the people living there had not been affected much by the war.

Cornwallis ordered Major Patrick Ferguson, commander of a company of Loyalist soldiers, to invade and take control of the "overmountain" territories. This direct threat aroused the independent pioneers to action.

On September 25, 1780, more than a thousand men from Virginia and North Carolina joined the settlers at Sycamore Shoals—now the town of Elizabethton, Tennessee. They set out on a ten-day, 180-mile (290-kilometer) march across the mountains to find Major Ferguson and his forces. At Kings Mountain, South Carolina, a one-hour battle resulted in the death or capture of all the Loyalist troops. Sir Henry Clinton, British commander-in-chief, called this battle the "first link in a chain of evils that . . . ended in the total loss of America."

LOVE OF INDEPENDENCE

Many of the early settlers in Tennessee were of Scotch-Irish descent. Their fathers and grandfathers had migrated from Scotland to northern Ireland, and from there to America, where they established homes in the colonies of Pennsylvania, Virginia, and North Carolina.

From there, seeking to get away from the colonial governments, they had pushed down through the valleys and over the mountains into wilderness territories. In their search for independence, settlers in East Tennessee lived under governments that changed forms eight times during a period of only twenty-seven years.

First they were part of the British colony of North Carolina, then in a land known as "Tributary to the Indians." Some settlers formed the independent Watauga Association. When the United States became independent, North Carolina claimed the Tennessee region first as the Washington District of North Carolina and then as Washington County, North Carolina.

For a variety of reasons, the Tennessee people were not satisfied to be governed by North Carolina. The state capital was far away and hard to reach, way over on the other side of the mountains. Also, it looked as if North Carolina would soon cede the territory to the United States government because the state could not protect its territory from the Indians. Delegates from three counties met in Jonesborough and formed a new state in 1784, called Frankland, land of the free. Later the name was changed to Franklin, in honor of Benjamin Franklin.

John Sevier, the highly respected military hero of the Battle of Kings Mountain, was elected governor of the newly self-proclaimed state. North Carolina, however, did not give up its claim to the territory, and its tax collectors continued to dispute the validity of Franklin. When Sevier's term as governor ended, in March 1788, no one was willing to run for the office and the young state quietly died. Once again, the Tennessee territory was part of North Carolina.

In 1790, the federal government set up the Territory of the United States South of the River Ohio. William Blount of North Carolina was appointed its governor.

By this time, various territories outside the boundaries of the original thirteen states were interested in achieving statehood for themselves. Vermont was admitted to statehood in 1791, Kentucky in 1792. Tennesseans also petitioned for statehood, and on June 1, 1796, theirs became the sixteenth state of the Union. John Sevier was the new state's first governor.

Sevier was popular with his people, who called him, affectionately, Chucky Jack. He served them for the next nineteen years, until his death: as governor for eleven years and as

Cherokee leader Sequoyah created a written alphabet of eighty-six characters for the Cherokee language and taught the Cherokees to read and write.

representative to the United States Congress for eight years. The new frontier settlements thrived and grew under his leadership as governor. Industry and agriculture developed rapidly, and many schools and churches were built.

A NATIVE AMERICAN GIANT

The Cherokee people, who for centuries inhabited much of the present-day southeastern United States, produced an amazing leader—Sequoyah. He was born shortly before the American Revolution in the valley of the lower Little Tennessee River, nestled in the shadow of the Great Smoky Mountains. The huge sequoia trees of California are named for this unusual man.

In his youth, Sequoyah was impressed with the ability of the white settlers to communicate with each other by putting symbols

In 1815, Andrew Jackson (on white horse) led the Tennessee volunteers to victory at the Battle of New Orleans. After the war, Jackson built a fine house, called The Hermitage, in Nashville (above).

on paper. In 1818, he decided that he would create a written alphabet for his own Cherokee language. His work took several years, and none of his friends took the task seriously.

Eventually, Sequoyah completed a system of eighty-six characters, each one representing a sound used in his native tongue. He taught them to his daughter, and together they demonstrated to his tribespeople the art of reading. In 1821, the Cherokee leaders adopted Sequoyah's alphabet. The Cherokees were thrilled with the new alphabet and quickly set to work learning how to read and write. They used whatever instruments they had to carve the symbols on leaves, bark, or pieces of wood.

Sequoyah's alphabet was a brilliant accomplishment. The world had not seen the invention of a new alphabet for five thousand years!

THREE FAMOUS SONS OF TENNESSEE

War heroes have often risen to political leadership in the United States. George Washington came to prominence as a general during the American Revolution, and America's next major conflict, the War of 1812, gave a Nashville lawyer named Andrew Jackson his opportunity to become a hero. During that war, he led a contingent of Tennessee volunteers in a campaign against the Creek Indians, who had been encouraged by the British to attack an American fort. Jackson and his volunteers broke the Creeks' power in 1814. Jackson's toughness under hardship earned him the nickname Old Hickory.

The Battle of New Orleans, in January 1815, was another brilliant victory for Jackson and the Tennessee volunteers. Jackson lost only about half a dozen of his men as contrasted with more than two thousand British casualties. Ironically, though, the battle was unnecessary because a peace treaty had been signed two weeks earlier. With no modern means of communication, the word had not yet reached New Orleans. Tennessee's nickname, the Volunteer State, comes from the bravery of the Tennessee volunteers during the War of 1812.

At the end of the war, Jackson went back to Nashville and built a fine house that he named The Hermitage. Before the War of 1812, he had had some political experience as a delegate to the state constitutional convention, as a member of both houses of Congress, and as a justice of the state supreme court.

The paths of two younger Tennesseans crossed those of Jackson during his battles against the Creeks. The names Sam Houston and Davy Crockett are nearly as well known in American history as is Andrew Jackson.

Sam Houston's family moved to Tennessee from Virginia when he was thirteen years old. Two years later, in 1808, Houston ran away from home and lived for nearly three years with a Cherokee tribe. In 1813, he joined Jackson's army in fighting the Creeks and became Jackson's lifelong friend.

Davy Crockett, meanwhile, was serving Jackson as a scout. Born in 1786 in Tennessee, Crockett was a skilled hunter and woodsman.

In 1823, Davy Crockett was elected to the state legislature; Sam Houston to the United States House of Representatives; and Andrew Jackson to the United States Senate once again. Four years later, Crockett went to Congress and Houston became Tennessee's governor.

Jackson's real ambition by this time was the presidency. He ran for that office in 1824, and although he was a popular favorite, he did not receive a majority of the votes in the electoral college. Four candidates were running, and while Jackson had more votes than any of the others, it was not a majority. The election, decided by the House of Representatives, went to John Quincy Adams.

Jackson resigned from the Senate in 1825 in order to prepare for a tough presidential battle in 1828. It was a bitterly fought campaign between Jackson and Adams, but Jackson won by more than two votes to one in the electoral college. His joy in the victory ended suddenly, however, when his wife died before his inauguration as seventh president of the United States.

Houston served as governor for only a short time. When his wife left him in 1829, he resigned as governor and moved to Texas, which was then part of Mexico. There he organized an army to free the territory from Mexican rule and became its commander-in-chief.

Davy Crockett, one of America's most famous frontiersmen, served in Congress for three terms. Crockett was a gifted storyteller and speaker, and he wrote three books about his own life and adventures. He was also quick-tempered and sharp-tongued. When Jackson became president, Crockett opposed his policies of moving the Indians off their land to make room for

Colorful soldier and politician Sam Houston resigned as governor of Tennessee in 1829 and moved to Texas. In 1836, he led the Army of Texas to victory in the Texas revolution, and later that year was elected the first president of the Republic of Texas.

white settlement. This stand was partially responsible for Crockett's defeat in 1835.

When his constituents failed to reelect him, Crockett reacted by saying they "could go to hell, I'm going to Texas." So he followed his friend Sam Houston to the western land, where he died along with 188 other members of the Army of Texas during the siege of the Alamo in 1836. Later that year, Houston led the Army of Texas to victory and was elected the first president of the Republic of Texas.

Chapter 5

THE VOLUNTEER STATE DEVELOPS

THE VOLUNTEER STATE DEVELOPS

The first six presidents had all come from wealthy families and lived in either Virginia or Massachusetts. Jackson, by contrast, had been born in a log cabin in 1767, had become an orphan at the age of fourteen, and grew up on the frontier. He was considered to be a "man of the people."

Through Jackson, the newly created western states such as Tennessee began to have an increasing influence on the national scene. Jackson was called the "people's president," and the twenty-year period following his election is known as the time of "the rise of the common man." It is also called the Age of Jackson by historians.

THE JACKSON PRESIDENCY

The nature of American government changed in several important ways while Andrew Jackson was president. Majority rule became the accepted principle of the country's system of government. Politicians brought representatives of the common people into government by appointing friends who had done them favors. This is known as the "spoils system."

President Jackson assumed much more power than his predecessors had. He fought with Congress for measures he believed would benefit ordinary people. The Internal Improvement Act of 1830 set aside money to develop the roads

Tennessean Andrew Jackson (right), elected president in 1828, is shown in the picture above on his way to his first inauguration.

and rivers of Tennessee, and of other states, for trade and transportation. Thus, Tennessee's farmers could get their cotton, wheat, and tobacco to market more cheaply. During and after Jackson's presidency, Tennessee was the most important state in the middle South.

Jackson's concern for the "common man," however, did not include women, blacks, or Native Americans. In 1818, ten years before being elected president, Andrew Jackson negotiated the Chickasaw Purchase, by which the Indians gave up their lands between the Tennessee and Mississippi rivers. He wanted the Indians to make room for white settlers to develop homes and towns.

While Jackson was president, the Indian Removal Act of 1830 was passed. This act enabled the government to force Indians in the East to move west of the Mississippi River. Most affected in Tennessee were the Cherokees. In 1831, about fourteen thousand of them were marched westward along a route that came to be known as the Trail of Tears. They endured unimaginable hardships along the way, and at least a fourth of them died before the rest reached Oklahoma.

During the administration of James K. Polk (left), the United States won a war with Mexico (right) and expanded its borders to include all the territory that would complete the first forty-eight states.

TENNESSEE POLITICS

The Democratic party was born with the election of Jackson in 1828. In 1832, for the first time, presidential candidates were chosen at national conventions instead of being nominated by state legislatures or by Congress.

The Whigs, the opposition party, became stronger in Tennessee as time went on. To counteract this, Jackson persuaded fellow-Tennessean James K. Polk to leave Washington, where he was Speaker of the House of Representatives, and go back home to work for the interests of the Democratic party.

Polk was elected governor of Tennessee in 1839 but served only one term. In 1844, he became the second Tennessean to be elected president of the United States—but the electors of his own state did not support him.

Soon after he took office, Polk stated that he had four goals for his administration: to reduce the tariff (the tax on imported goods), establish an independent treasury, settle the Oregon boundary dispute, and acquire the California territory. All of these goals were achieved.

Polk tried to buy California from Mexico, but did not succeed. At the same time, the two countries were in disagreement over the boundary between Mexico and Texas. The difficulties led to a war, which ended in an American victory and the acquisition of much land in present-day California, Nevada, and Utah, as well as part of Arizona, Colorado, New Mexico, and Wyoming.

Though Tennessee's quota for volunteers to fight in the Mexican War was only 2,800, about 30,000 answered the call. The Volunteer State, the nickname given to the state during the War of 1812, lived up to its reputation.

ECONOMIC GROWTH AND SLAVERY IN TENNESSEE

Railroads began operation in Tennessee in 1842, and by 1860, an effective network of rail routes crisscrossed the state. Telegraphic communication was set up in 1848. Along with improved transportation and communication came industrial development. By 1860, the manufacture of flour, cotton fabric, woolens, iron, and railroad and farm equipment were among the state's top ten industries.

The state's economy was based on agricultural products, however, except for the iron produced in Middle Tennessee. Until the 1860s, agriculture enjoyed a period of prosperity throughout the state, but types of farming differed widely in the state's three sections.

In East Tennessee, most of the farms were small, family-run establishments. The uneven terrain and the rocky soil were not conducive to creating large plantations. Thus, in East Tennessee most farmers owned very few, if any, slaves. Many of the slaves who had been brought into this part of the state by some of the earliest settlers had earned their freedom by helping in the American Revolution. The Tennessee constitution of 1796 allowed them to vote and to hold property.

Even though many of the blacks in East Tennessee were free, they were quite rigidly segregated. Some were members of white churches, mostly Methodist and Baptist, but they were required to sit in balconies or at the back of the church.

Many families in Middle and West Tennessee had come west from Virginia and North Carolina to establish tobacco and cotton plantations. They brought their slaves with them to work in the fields and the iron furnaces.

Because of these different economic needs, attitudes toward slavery also differed in the three regions. Feelings were based on economic issues as well as moral ones.

East Tennessee settlers who had come from Pennsylvania, many of them Quakers, were opposed to slavery. In 1815, some of those Quakers formed the Tennessee Society for Promoting the Manumission (freeing) of Slaves. Two early antislavery newspapers were published in the area.

One movement favored removing all blacks to Liberia, on the West Coast of Africa. The American Colonization Society was formed to promote that goal. Andrew Jackson served for a while as the society's vice-president. By 1867, about six thousand blacks had been taken to Liberia.

Tennessee's constitution of 1834 took away the right of free blacks to vote. No civil rights were given to "people of color." One participant in the constitutional convention said that when the new United States Constitution referred to "we the people," it really meant only "we the free white people."

In 1840, blacks—both slave and free—made up only 9.4 percent of the population of East Tennessee. In Middle Tennessee, they

The American
Colonization
Society, whose
goal was to
remove all free
blacks to a new
colony in Liberia,
saw the first
such group leave
on the Liberian
ship *Azor* in 1822.

made up 26.5 percent of the population; and in West Tennessee, more than 30 percent. In the cotton-plantation counties of the southwest, blacks were in the majority.

Between 1810 and 1840, the slave population in the state increased by more than 300 percent. There was a growing fear of slave uprisings. Laws were passed that made distributing abolitionist literature or making abolitionist speeches punishable by prison sentences of five to twenty years. In 1859, the legislature actually considered a bill requiring free blacks to either leave the state or be enslaved.

The 1850s were years of high prices for cotton and tobacco, leading to the opening of more land and the need for even more slave labor. Slaves became more valuable. By 1860, slavery was an important economic institution in the more populated parts of the state, while still not popular in the mountains.

TENNESSEE BECOMES A HOUSE DIVIDED

Tennessee voters were not happy when Abraham Lincoln was elected president, but they were in no hurry to secede from the Union. Lincoln's Republican party opposed extending slavery into the new western territories. Southern slaveholders felt that each state and territory should decide for itself whether it would be slave or free. The southerners were also afraid that Lincoln might restrict their right to have slaves in the South.

In February 1861, six of the southern states organized the Confederate States of America. During that same month, a vote was held in Tennessee on whether to hold a convention to decide between staying with the Union or joining the Confederacy. At that time, the pro-Union advocates were the winners.

However, when the shelling of Fort Sumter in South Carolina, in April, made war between North and South inevitable, feelings changed. Tennessee held a general election in June to decide the question of secession. The vote was more than two-to-one in favor of separation. Nearly all the pro-Union votes came from East Tennessee.

A few days after the vote to secede, people from twenty-six counties in East Tennessee drew up a petition to separate from Tennessee and form their own state. Although this never happened, many East Tennesseans remained fiercely loyal to the Union and did all they could to help the Union cause.

One East Tennessee citizen who chose to remain loyal to the Union was a United States senator—a tailor from Greeneville— named Andrew Johnson. In March 1862, President Lincoln appointed Johnson military governor of Tennessee. Although Johnson was a Democrat and Lincoln was a Republican, they were nominated as running mates in the campaign of 1864.

This battery of black troops was part of the victorious Union force that fought against the Confederacy at Nashville.

The people of East Tennessee had great respect for Johnson, but people in the rest of the state, viewing him as part of the enemy camp, thoroughly hated him. He was a man of courage who dared to speak out publicly against his own state's secession. He was the only southern member of the Senate who did so.

BROTHER AGAINST BROTHER

During the Civil War, Tennessee again produced a great number of volunteers for military service: 55,000 to 70,000 Union soldiers, including 20,000 blacks who fought with the Union; and 100,000 to 135,000 Confederate soldiers. Some families had soldiers in both armies.

The war was especially bloody in this state. More of the fiercest battles were fought in Tennessee than in any other state except Virginia. General Ulysses S. Grant's strategy for the Union's

The Civil War Battle of Limestone Station is reenacted at the Tipton-Haynes Historical Farm.

western campaign was to gain control of the rivers and railroads. Controlling the Cumberland, Tennessee, and Mississippi rivers in Tennessee and the railroad centers of Chattanooga and Nashville was essential for the success of Grant's plan.

Thousands of lives were lost at Shiloh, Stones River, Chattanooga, Franklin, Fort Donelson, and Nashville. Union forces captured Memphis in June 1862. This was a crucial victory because the city was an important cotton market and a strategic port on the Mississippi River.

Armies crossed Tennessee many times, ruining the countryside and stealing supplies as they went. But in the midst of the horrible devastation and strife that divided hundreds of families, guests at one Chattanooga wedding put aside their differences to celebrate the marriage. The wedding party was attended by soldiers, deserters, spies, and citizens from both sides. According to an eyewitness account, "scarcely a harsh word was uttered during the whole night; all danced together as if nothing was wrong, and parted mutually the next morning, each party marching off separately."

Such harmonious interludes were rare, not only during the war but for years after it ended. The intense differences of opinion hindered relationships among neighbors for more than one generation. Even local churches were split along pro-Union and pro-Confederacy lines. In a few small towns in northeastern Tennessee, there are still two churches of the same denomination that trace their division to the Civil War days.

Two historical markers stand in front of the courthouse in Greeneville today. One commemorates the heroism of Confederate General John Morgan; the other is dedicated to the memory of Greene County volunteers who enlisted in the Union army.

RECONSTRUCTION UNDER TENNESSEE'S THIRD PRESIDENT

With the end of the war and the assassination of President Abraham Lincoln, both in April 1865, Vice-President Andrew Johnson of Tennessee succeeded to the presidency. Congress was dominated at that time by a group of Republicans known as Radicals because they wanted to punish the South severely for having fought against the Union.

Johnson had made certain public threats that pleased the Radicals; they considered him to be one of them. Soon after he became president, however, Johnson's mood changed. He realized that the South was in terrible shape. Tennessee's economy, along with that of the other Confederate states, was in ruins. Factories had been destroyed, farms had been trampled, the roads were crumbling, and the railroads had been torn up. As a man whose own early years had been both humble and difficult, Johnson's natural sympathy for the underdog was aroused. He proposed a humane policy of Reconstruction that would bring the rebelling states back into the Union.

In June 1865, the president issued a proclamation to bring Tennessee back into the Union. But the Radicals in Congress held off its readmission until March 1866. Nevertheless, Tennessee was the first Confederate state to be readmitted. Congress refused to go along with other presidential measures and passed Reconstruction measures of its own over Johnson's veto.

Disputes and differences between Congress and the executive branch became so serious that the House of Representatives impeached Johnson (charged him with misconduct). After a trial, the president could be removed from office. The two-month-long trial resulted in an acquittal—by one vote. The Senate had failed to convict Johnson. He is the only president in history who has suffered the humiliation of an impeachment trial.

Johnson's popularity was at a low ebb then, and his political influence was gone. He continued to veto the tough Reconstruction measures enacted by Congress, but they were easily passed over his veto.

On Christmas Day, 1868, only three months before his term was over, President Johnson issued a proclamation giving a complete pardon to all southerners who had taken part in the Civil War. While the proclamation had little real force, it demonstrated his desire to bring about a real peace between the two sides.

When Johnson retired to Tennessee, he was more discredited than any other president had been at the end of a term. He remained active in politics, and ran twice, unsuccessfully, for Congress. In 1875, he did win a seat in the Senate, but died of a stroke only a few weeks after attending one short session.

During Reconstruction, Tennessee's newly freed blacks made great political, economic, and educational gains. The Freedmen's Bureau, which was established by Congress in 1865, set up seventy-five schools for blacks. Fisk University was established for blacks in 1866 by the American Missionary Association. Many blacks held political positions and started businesses.

Many whites in Tennessee opposed the Radicals' plans for Reconstruction. Some of them, under the leadership of Confederate General Nathan Bedford Forrest, formed the Ku Klux Klan in 1866 in Pulaski, Tennessee. Forrest was called the Grand Wizard. During the night, the Klansmen would ride out wearing white hoods and robes, their horses covered with white sheets, to terrorize blacks and keep them from exercising their newly won rights. In 1869, Tennessee passed laws against the Klan and the group disbanded.

RECOVERY

The next few decades in Tennessee were marked by a number of colorful and intense political races. In 1886, brothers Alfred A. and Robert L. Taylor campaigned against each other for the governorship in a race known as the War of the Roses.

Mining for coal, iron, and copper grew in importance in southeastern Tennessee. Factories producing flour, woolens, paper, and cottonseed oil were established throughout the state.

As the nineteenth century drew to an end, Tennessee celebrated three important events. In 1892, in West Tennessee, an impressive ceremony marked the opening of the three-mile cantilever bridge over the Mississippi River at Memphis. In 1895, in East Tennessee, the Chickamauga and Chattanooga National Military Park was dedicated. This park is on the site of the battles of Lookout Mountain, Missionary Ridge, Chickamauga, and Chattanooga. From May to December 1897, Nashville, in Middle Tennessee, hosted Tennessee's centennial exposition.

Chapter 6
THE TWENTIETH CENTURY

THE TWENTIETH CENTURY

As Tennessee entered the twentieth century, two major issues in the state were temperance and woman suffrage. The Tennessee Anti-Saloon League and the Women's Christian Temperance Union campaigned vigorously to prohibit the manufacture, sale, and use of alcoholic beverages. In 1909, a statewide prohibition law was passed and Tennessee became a dry state. Between 1919 and 1933, while a national prohibition amendment to the United States Constitution was in effect, the rest of the United States joined Tennessee.

The cause of woman suffrage, however, had to wait until World War I was over. In 1920, Tennessee became the thirty-sixth—and deciding—state to ratify the Nineteenth Amendment to the United States Constitution that gave women the right to vote.

WORLD WAR I AND AFTER

While the United States was involved in World War I (1914-18), Tennessee once again lived up to its reputation as the Volunteer State. Close to 100,000 Tennesseans enlisted. Sergeant Alvin C. York of Pall Mall was America's most famous hero from that war.

In addition to men, Tennessee also contributed supplies for the war effort. Tennessee's factory workers increased their production of goods such as cotton and woolen cloth for uniforms and aluminum. A factory that produced smokeless powder for guns was built near Nashville.

World War I, in many ways, marked the end of an old era and the beginning of a new one in the United States. In the 1920s, however, the way of life in Tennessee had not changed much. Strangers seldom intruded deep into the hills and "hollers" of Appalachia. People there took for granted that there was only one way to think about almost any subject because no one ever challenged the old ways and ideas. In 1925, a small town 38 miles (61 kilometers) north of Chattanooga was the scene of one of the most celebrated challenges of an old idea ever witnessed.

THE SCOPES TRIAL

An upsurge in religious fervor took place in the 1920s. Most Tennesseans were fundamentalists. They believed that every word in the Bible was true, not to be denied, interpreted to mean anything different, or translated into more modern language.

A Tennessee legislator who held these fundamentalist views read parts of a book called *The Origin of Species*, which had been written by an English scientist named Charles Darwin in 1859. Darwin proposed that the world and humankind were not created in seven days, as the book of Genesis relates, but were instead products of an evolution that had taken place over millions of years.

The legislator, incensed at this "heresy," introduced a bill in the assembly making it illegal for any teacher in any public school in the state to "teach any theory that denies the story of the Divine Creation of man as taught in the Bible, and to teach instead that man has descended from a lower order of animals."

A few weeks after this bill became law, a group of community leaders in the little town of Dayton decided that the law should be tested in court, and persuaded the local high-school biology

Eloquent defense lawyer Clarence Darrow (above) in action at the Scopes trial

teacher, John Scopes, to be the defendant in a test case. One of the leaders, the chairman of the local school board, called the *Chattanooga Times* and told the reporter they had arrested a teacher for teaching evolution.

Suddenly, Dayton was the center of worldwide attention. The eight-day trial, which took place in July 1925, was attended by hundreds of reporters, some of them famous in their own right.

Two nationally prominent lawyers presented the two sides of the case. William Jennings Bryan, a politician who had been the unsuccessful Democratic candidate for the presidency three times, represented the state. Known as a "silver-tongued orator," he was a religious fundamentalist. Scopes was defended by Clarence Darrow, a brilliant debater and defense lawyer.

The outcome of the "monkey trial," as it was nicknamed, was not of much consequence. Scopes was found guilty and fined

$100, but the Tennessee Supreme Court set aside the verdict because of a legal error. The law remained on the books for the next forty years, though most educators paid little attention to it. The story of the trial itself, however, and its two main figures—Bryan and Darrow—has been told and retold in books, plays, and a movie.

THE TENNESSEE VALLEY AUTHORITY

The 1920s were a period of prosperity for some Americans, but in rural Tennessee, small farmers were still scratching out an existence threatened by poverty, poor nutrition, and inadequate housing. In the valley of the Tennessee River, average personal income was only 45 percent of the national average. When the stock market crashed in 1929 and the Great Depression followed, Tennesseans were hit with economic disaster sooner and more crushingly than most of the rest of the country.

When Franklin Delano Roosevelt became president of the United States in 1933, he immediately started a number of programs to correct the problems caused by the Great Depression. His programs, overall, were known as the New Deal. The most far-reaching program of all, and the one that had the greatest effect on Tennesseans, was the Tennessee Valley Authority (TVA), created by an act of Congress in May 1933. The newly created government corporation was charged with "planning for the proper use, conservation, and development of the natural resources of the Tennessee River drainage basin and its adjoining territory for the general social and economic welfare of the nation."

The agency was to control the vast waterways of the Tennessee River and its tributaries by building, or buying, and managing a series of dams. Today there are thirty-nine of these dams. When the rivers were harnessed, the TVA had accomplished its many goals. These goals were to control floods, to improve navigation, to manufacture inexpensive electrical power, to develop agriculture and industry, to conserve natural resources, and to create recreational facilities.

Furthermore, with its headquarters in Knoxville, the TVA became a major creator of jobs for Tennesseans, and it attracted well-educated technicians and scientists to the area. The agency has been a major factor in changing East Tennessee from the most backward, isolated, poverty-stricken section of the state into an equal partner with the other two "states of Tennessee."

WORLD WAR II

The United States' entry into World War II in 1941 once again made East Tennessee a major player on the national—indeed, international—scene, though for several years its role was cloaked in deep secrecy. President Roosevelt and several of his military and scientific advisors were convinced that Germany was working to create a more destructive weapon than the world had ever seen—an atomic bomb. American leaders felt it was critical to beat the Germans to their goal.

The plan to produce an atomic bomb within a three-year period, approved by the president in 1942, was called the Manhattan Project. Three secret sites were chosen for the work to be done. One of them was on a hillside known as Black Oak Ridge, on the Clinch River near Knoxville, in East Tennessee.

The total story of the building of an entire town, going about the business of creating an atomic bomb and keeping the entire project secret, reads like a thrilling spy mystery. The Army Corps

It wasn't until after the war that Oak Ridge workers learned that they had been working on the atomic bomb.

of Engineers, in charge of building the new city, wasted little time. In a period of five months, they bought up 56,000 acres (22,663 hectares) of land. Old-time residents were forced to sell land that had been in their families for generations. Three whole villages were simply eliminated. By the spring of 1945, a town with homes, shopping areas, and other facilities for a population of 75,000 had been built.

The extent to which Oak Ridge's secret was kept was amazing. The world's first atomic bomb was dropped on Hiroshima on August 6, 1945, and the great majority of Oak Ridge residents were as surprised as was the rest of the world. Only then did they realize their part in the extraordinary endeavor that was to change the world for all time.

Tennessee played a major role in wartime, and a Tennessee politician and statesman played a major role in laying plans for a lasting peace. Cordell Hull served as secretary of state under President Roosevelt from 1933 until poor health forced him to resign in 1944. Before his resignation, Secretary Hull drew up the first plans for the United Nations organization. For this and his other efforts on behalf of world peace, he was awarded the 1945 Nobel Peace Prize.

SINCE WORLD WAR II

Between 1950 and 1970, large numbers of Tennessee's people moved off the farms and into towns and cities. Blacks left rural Tennessee in even greater numbers than whites. Some went to cities within the state, others to metropolitan areas in the North and West. In general, the shift from farms to cities and from agriculture to industry has brought greater prosperity to Tennessee. In 1953, the Tennessee Industrial and Agricultural Development Commission was established. Within ten years it created a 28 percent increase in manufacturing jobs.

Politics in Tennessee also underwent changes after World War II. Since the early 1900s, Edward Crump had been the political boss of Memphis and had controlled Democratic party politics within the state. In 1948, Estes Kefauver, a Democrat, ran for the United States Senate and won in spite of Crump's opposition. This election marked the beginning of the end of Crump's power.

During the 1950s, the Republican party began to gain more backing in the state. In 1966, Howard Baker was elected to the United States Senate—the first Republican to win in a Tennessee statewide race since 1920.

CIVIL RIGHTS

In 1954, when the Supreme Court handed down its historic decision that segregated public schools were unconstitutional and should be integrated, white southerners were irate. Nearly all the southern senators signed a statement called the Southern Manifesto, in which they stated their opposition to obeying what the Supreme Court had decided was the law of the land.

One of Tennessee's senators, Estes Kefauver, courageously refused to sign the manifesto. This action caused many of his constituents to become his enemies.

There were a number of confrontations, both in the streets and in the courts, before Tennessee's schools were integrated. In 1964, a federal court ordered the Tennessee legislature to redraw its legislative districts so that blacks and whites would have equal representation. The boundaries were redrawn in 1965. Tennessee escaped much of the violence over civil rights that plagued other southern states during the 1960s.

However, on April 4, 1968, Memphis was the scene of a tragic event that became the single most important symbol of the civil-rights struggle. The popular and respected leader of the movement, Nobel Peace Prizewinner Martin Luther King, Jr., was assassinated by a sniper while visiting the city to take part in a campaign to improve working conditions for the city's garbage workers.

RECENT TRENDS

Tennessee's main problems in the 1980s were a low standard of living among many of its people, a low literacy rate, and insufficient tax revenues. Tennesseans are determined, however, to turn these problems around. The state has been a national leader in educational reform since the early 1980s. Tax revenues should increase as more industries and jobs come to Tennessee.

An assembly line at the Nissan plant in Smyrna

During the 1980s, Tennessee witnessed a surge in industrial development. Knoxville hosted a world's fair in 1982 that helped promote tourism throughout the state. Also in 1982, Nissan Motors opened an automobile manufacturing plant in Smyrna. At the time, it was the largest foreign investment in the United States.

In 1985, the Tennessee-Tombigbee Waterway, which connects the Tennessee River and the Gulf of Mexico, was completed. This waterway should attract more industries to the state and increase Tennessee's interstate and intrastate trade.

A new General Motors automobile plant, which should create about twenty thousand jobs, is scheduled to open in Spring Hill in 1990. Other support industries are coming into the state as a result of these occurrences. Tennessee is well on its way to the twenty-first century.

Chapter 7

GOVERNMENT AND THE ECONOMY

GOVERNMENT AND THE ECONOMY

Tennessee's first constitution was adopted at a convention in Knoxville in 1796, just before the territory was admitted to the Union as a state. New constitutions were written at conventions in Nashville in 1834 and 1870. Tennessee's constitution stood unchanged until 1953, when it was amended to allow the governor to serve a four-year term. The most recent amendments were made in 1978. They limited the state's spending and allowed a governor to serve two consecutive terms. Tennessee's constitution has changed as the peoples' views on government and economics have changed.

GOVERNMENT

The state has three branches of government, similar to those of the federal government. The legislative branch consists of a general assembly made up of two houses—a senate and a house of representatives. State senators are elected by popular vote for a four-year term; members of the house for a two-year term. The house has ninety-nine members, the senate thirty-three.

The second branch of government is the executive. The Tennessee state constitution places the "supreme executive power" of the state with the governor. The governor is elected by popular vote to serve a four-year term and to administer the laws enacted by the legislature. Twenty-one cabinet-level departments,

Courts that convene in the Washington County Courthouse in Jonesborough are part of Tennessee's judicial branch of government.

employing more than thirty-five thousand people, make up the executive branch. The governor appoints the cabinet members who head up these departments. The lieutenant governor is the speaker of the senate.

Three officers in the executive branch are elected by a joint session of the house and senate. These are the secretary of state, who is elected for a four-year term; and the comptroller of the treasury and the state treasurer, each of whom serves for two years. The attorney general is selected by the state supreme court for an eight-year term.

Tennessee's judicial branch, the third basic division of the state's government, is headed by a five-person supreme court. Members of the supreme court are elected by popular vote to serve eight-year terms. It is the responsibility of the judicial branch to interpret the state's laws. The next courts are intermediate appellate courts, and below them are the general trial courts. A fourth level consists of certain courts of limited jurisdiction, such as municipal, probate, and juvenile courts. All Tennessee judges are elected to eight-year terms.

The University of the South (above) and Vanderbilt University
(right) are among Tennessee's institutions of higher learning.

COUNTY AND LOCAL GOVERNMENT

Tennessee has ninety-five counties, each governed by a county
executive and district magistrates. The county government
administers elections, collects taxes and fees, issues licenses,
settles wills and estates, registers property titles, promotes public
health and library services, and enforces education laws.

Most of the state's cities are governed by a mayor and a city
council. Twelve cities have adopted home rule. They operate
under their own charter and are not controlled by the state
legislature.

EDUCATION

Tennessee's 140 public school systems serve some 850,000
students and employ nearly 48,000 teachers and other
professionals. About 200,000 students—more than half of those

enrolled in grades seven through twelve—are in vocational education programs.

Special educational services are available to all gifted and handicapped children. Some of these students are educated in one of five special schools governed by the state board of education. Summer residential programs administered by the state are held on college campuses for gifted and talented high-school students.

The state university and community college system of Tennessee administers six state universities, ten community colleges, four state technical institutes, and twenty-six area vocational-technical schools. The University of Tennessee system has campuses in Knoxville, Chattanooga, Martin, and Memphis.

There are more than two dozen private degree-granting colleges and universities in the state, most with enrollments of fewer than twenty-five hundred students. A notable exception is Nashville's Vanderbilt University, established in 1873, which serves nearly nine thousand undergraduate and graduate students.

TRANSPORTATION

There are four major hubs of transportation in Tennessee: Memphis, Nashville, Knoxville, and Chattanooga. Major highways and railroads meet and cross in these cities. All have busy airports and all are located on important rivers.

Railroads have been important in the state for nearly 150 years, but today the only city with passenger rail service is Memphis, which is a stop on the Chicago-New Orleans route. Most rail lines carry only freight.

The largest and busiest airport in the state is Memphis International Airport. More than 1 million passengers use this airport each year.

Memphis is one of Tennessee's major hubs of transportation.

Of Tennessee's 84,351 miles (135,746 kilometers) of roads, 1,062 miles (1,709 kilometers) are interstate highways. Interstates 40 and 81 cross the state from east to west; Interstates 24, 65, and 75, from north to south. The Natchez Trace Parkway, leading south from Nashville to Natchez, Mississippi, is a scenic highway administered by the National Park Service. It follows a historic Indian and pioneer trail.

With 1,000 miles (1,609 kilometers) of navigable waterways, Tennessee's rivers are still an important means of transportation. Tennessee has direct access to the Mississippi River and access to the Ohio River via the Cumberland and Tennessee rivers. The Tennessee-Tombigbee Waterway provides a direct passage for vessels between the Tennessee River and the Gulf of Mexico.

COMMUNICATION

Major newspapers in the state are the *News-Free Press*, published in Chattanooga; the *Journal* and *News-Sentinel*, in Knoxville; the

Livestock accounts for more than half of the state's income from agriculture. Tobacco (above) is one of the major crops produced.

Commercial Appeal, in Memphis; and the *Banner* and *Tennessean*, in Nashville. The state has about thirty daily newspapers. Nashville is a major publishing center for religious material and music. Several dozen trade publications are also issued from there.

There are 278 radio stations in the state, 29 television stations, and more than 140 cable systems. The state telecommunications office provides educational services for six noncommercial television stations.

AGRICULTURE AND ANIMAL HUSBANDRY

Livestock and livestock products account for more than half the state's income from agriculture, with meat animals—especially cattle and hogs—at the top of the list. Breeding and raising the famous Tennessee Walking Horse is another source of income. This horse is bred to carry its rider at a comfortable gait for long periods of time. Poultry, eggs, and milk products are also important.

Gibson guitars are produced in a Nashville factory.

Until the early 1960s, cotton was Tennessee's leading crop, but today soybeans and tobacco tie for first in percent of income— 15 percent each. Cotton ranks third in value, with corn in fourth place. Other important crops are hay, wheat, tomatoes, snap beans, cabbage, potatoes, sweet potatoes, apples, peaches, and strawberries.

MINING

Tennessee ranks twenty-ninth among the fifty states in mineral production and leads the states in the production of zinc. Copper, iron, lead, manganese, and gold are other principal Tennessee metals. The state's greatest mining income comes from coal. Marble, portland cement, sand and gravel, and stone are the major nonmetal products.

BUSINESS AND INDUSTRY

In addition to the state's new automobile manufacturing industry around Nashville, chemicals, food and food products,

Musical recording is a major industry in Nashville.

electric and electronic equipment, machinery, clothing, and furniture are produced throughout Tennessee.

Printing and publishing are important businesses in Nashville and Kingsport, and Nashville is also a major insurance center. Higher education and health services employ large numbers of people in Nashville and Memphis.

Musical recording, television production, and live entertainment are industries that bring income both from goods sold and from the large number of visitors attracted to Nashville. Nashville is also the state's convention center.

One of the world's largest hotel-motel chains, Holiday Inn, is headquartered in Memphis. Federal Express, a company that pioneered overnight delivery of mail and packages, also makes its home there.

Chapter 8

CULTURE AND RECREATION

CULTURE AND RECREATION

Tennessee has a rich cultural heritage. The capital city of Nashville, with its classical Greek public buildings, is known as the Athens of the South. Most of Tennessee's contributions to the arts, however, have not been in the classical forms. Regional literature, handicrafts, and music—from country and western to blues and from bluegrass to rock and roll—are among the gifts that Tennessee's writers and artists have given the state and the entire country.

LITERATURE

Nashville has been called the Athens of the South because of its long-standing reputation for cultural and intellectual leadership. In the 1920s and 1930s, a number of young poets and writers, some of them connected with Vanderbilt University, were writing and publishing.

The most famous member of this group was Robert Penn Warren, who went on to win two Pulitzer Prizes, one for a novel, *All the King's Men,* and one for a collection of poetry. The South was the scene of many of his novels. A Rhodes scholar, Warren also wrote textbooks on poetry and fiction.

Warren and three other poets formed a group called the Fugitives, who published works of criticism. They were reformers who wanted to preserve and promote the best of southern traditions.

Alex Haley, author of *Roots: The Saga of an American Family*

Another prizewinning Tennessee writer was James Agee, author of the novel *A Death in the Family*. The story, which opens with a Knoxville scene, was later made into a play, and then a motion picture. For the first time, the Pulitzer Prize was awarded for both the original novel and the play that was based on it.

Roark Bradford, a white writer, wrote stories about southern blacks, many of them with Biblical themes. One of them, *Ol' Man Adam and His Chillun*, published in 1928, was later dramatized in a highly successful and acclaimed Broadway production called *Green Pastures*.

Tennessee has also produced several noted black writers who have made significant contributions to the field of black studies. Dr. Arna Bontemps, at one time author-in-residence at Fisk University, published more than twenty books about the history, literature, and folklore of blacks.

Alex Haley, who grew up in Tennessee, wrote *Roots: The Saga of an American Family*, a best-selling book that was adapted for a television miniseries. It traces the history of a black family from its preslavery days in Africa. When first telecast, the series had a larger viewing audience than any other similar television series.

Wilma Dykeman is one of Tennessee's best-known contemporary writers of stories and historical works about the state. One literary authority has pointed out that a number of Tennessee writers have written not only about their region, but about family life in the South. They use the theme of how family life and family values shape society.

ART

William Edward West was Tennessee's first professional artist. He came from Philadelphia in the early 1800s and made his home in Nashville. Mainly a portrait painter, he also illustrated a book for his close friend Washington Irving.

One of Tennessee's most famous landscape painters was James Cameron, who came from Scotland to Chattanooga. *A View of the Bluff and Valley*, painted in 1859, shows his close attention to realistic detail. Another European who came to Tennessee was Melchior Thoni, a Swiss woodcarver and cabinet maker. In 1869, he settled in Nashville and began sculpting in wood. One of his most ambitious projects was carving the first wooden animals for a merry-go-round.

During the 1890s, George de Forest Brush of Shelbyville and Frank Wilbert Stokes of Nashville gained fame. Brush's most important works were of Indian life—*Silence Broken* and *Mourning Her Brave*—and his portraits of his wife and children—*In the Garden* and *Family Group.* The last two are in the Metropolitan Museum of Art in New York and the Chicago Art Institute, respectively. Stokes was an artist who accompanied expeditions to

Greenland and the North Pole. *Return of Admiral Byrd from the North Pole* is one of his most famous paintings of that expedition.

In the 1930s, Aaron K. Douglas, a black artist, painted murals on the walls of Fisk University's library. They show in a symbolic way the history of blacks. Another black artist in Nashville, William Edmunson, sculpted tombstones with figures from the Bible. His work was exhibited at the Museum of Modern Art in New York.

Other twentieth-century Tennessee sculptors were Harold Cash of Chattanooga and Thomas Mims of Nashville. Both had their works exhibited in New York.

MOUNTAIN MUSIC

In East Tennessee, the first settlers, whose families had originally come from England and Scotland, brought their traditional music and instruments with them. They sang and played the folk ballads that had been handed down from generation to generation since Elizabethan times. Because many of these mountain people lived in isolation, without any outside influences, the ballads were preserved with their original form almost intact.

Along with the early songs, local composers and rhymesters in the nineteenth century wrote songs about current events and famous people. These later ballads were similar in sound and in theme to the older ones. Over the years, these became a part of the repertoire of mountain balladeers.

Another type of music popular in Tennessee life in the nineteenth century was religious, or gospel, music. People enjoyed getting together for "singing conventions," a time for socializing, picnicking, and enthusiastically praising the Lord with lively

Tennessee artisans still make beautiful handmade dulcimers, a traditional Appalachian instrument.

hymns. Blacks had their own gospel songs such as "When the Lord Called Moses" and "I'm Troubled in Mind." In the twentieth century, the James D. Vaughan Company of Lawrenceburg published, recorded, and broadcast gospel music.

Ballads were sometimes sung accompanied by a fiddle. Fiddle music was the major accompaniment at country dances. Fiddling contests are still held in Knoxville. Harmonicas were also in common use, and during the late nineteenth century, banjo "pickin'" became more and more widespread.

BLUEGRASS MUSIC

Most early country musicians were soloists, but by the 1920s string bands consisting of fiddles, banjos, guitars, and an occasional mandolin or bass viol began to spring up in Tennessee.

Part of the Johnny Cash exhibit at the Country Music Hall of Fame, in Nashville

Bluegrass music has its roots in these early string bands. It is characterized by banjo music played in a rapid style, along with the vocal sounds of early mountain balladeers.

East Tennessee is regarded as the center of bluegrass music. Radio and television stations in Knoxville, Bristol, and Johnson City were early outlets for bluegrass artists.

THE NASHVILLE SOUND

When radio appeared in the 1920s, the folk songs and bluegrass music of East Tennessee were brought to people all around the country who had never heard it before.

Record companies soon started recording country music. Several Tennessee musicians became popular stars almost overnight. The first recordings of "hillbilly," or country, music

Dolly Parton (above) and Loretta Lynn (right) are two of the many country singers who got their start with Nashville's Grand Ole Opry.

were made in Bristol in 1927. Some of the earliest artists to record there were the Carter Family and Jimmie Rodgers.

By 1925, Nashville's National Life and Accident Insurance Company started its own station—WSM, named for the insurance company's motto, "We Shield Millions." The first programs offered light classical music, ballroom dance orchestras, and lectures. Since the 1,000-watt station was reaching a large rural audience outside Nashville, "Barn Dance," a new program featuring folk music, was aired on Saturday nights. In 1927, the show received the famous name it has carried for more than six decades: the Grand Ole Opry.

In those early days, musicians, most of whom had regular jobs and played or sang as a hobby, were happy to play on the radio for $10 to $15 a night. Today, Nashville is full of mansions built by the musicians who have become millionaires through their

Minnie Pearl and Roy Acuff at the Grand Ole Opry

work on records, radio, and television; in the movies; and from live performances.

The Grand Ole Opry was only the beginning for Nashville, now popularly called Music City, USA. Following World War II, the recording business began to be an important part of the Nashville scene. New studio techniques were used to create what became known as "the Nashville sound." The terms "folk" and "hillbilly" were replaced by the words "country and western" to describe this uniquely American music.

In 1972, the owners of the Grand Ole Opry opened Opryland USA, a family entertainment park, on the outskirts of Nashville. The number and professional quality of live musical performances are the park's primary appeal. In the 1980s, they added another dimension to their entertainment empire with the establishment of The Nashville Network on cable television.

MEMPHIS IS HEARD

Musical traditions in West Tennessee had a totally different origin from the ballads that East Tennesseans grew up with. On the huge cotton plantations of the area, many slaves developed a musical form known as the blues. While they worked, they sang songs that had a definite beat that helped establish a rhythm for repetitious tasks such as chopping cotton. The melodies were often in a minor key, which gave the tune a mournful sound. The blues are a subdivision of the musical form known as jazz.

Jazz is undoubtedly descended in part from the musical heritage brought from Africa by the slaves. Today, however, jazz is generally regarded as the only musical form that originated in the United States.

Two strains of jazz that featured the piano—ragtime and honky-tonk—came upriver from the bars and riverboat saloons of New Orleans. The vocal work songs of the West Tennessee plantations mingled with these jazz forms in Memphis, where a musician named W. C. Handy was composing and performing. His compositions, including "Beale Street Blues," "Memphis Blues," and "St. Louis Blues," gave him the title Father of the Blues. His work and that of blues singer Bessie Smith gave Memphis a permanent place in the musical world as the center of the blues.

In the beginning, blues music was performed almost exclusively by black performers. As time went on, some white singers took it up, added a faster beat, and developed a style that came to be called rhythm and blues.

In the 1950s, a number of singers were making records in Memphis. One of them, a young Mississippi truck driver named Elvis Presley, combined the styles of country and western music

Above: Elvis Presley, originator of rock and roll, was one of the most popular entertainers in history. Left: A saxophone player at Libertyland, in Memphis

with current rhythm and blues and came up with a new form of American popular music known as rock and roll. Presley's phenomenal climb to fame was amazing, and before long his records were being played all over the world.

MORE TENNESSEE MUSICIANS

Tennessee's influence on American music is greatest in the fields of country and popular music, but the state has produced its share of other fine musical groups as well.

Two colleges have enjoyed an enduring prominence in music. The School of Music of George Peabody College for Teachers, in Nashville, is one of the strongest privately supported schools of its type in the nation. It has trained many outstanding music teachers

In the 1870s, the Fisk Jubilee Singers made a fund-raising tour of the United States and Europe to raise money for the first permanent building on the Fisk University campus.

and furnishes well-educated candidates for careers in musical recording. Charles Bryan, former professor of music at Peabody, won a Guggenheim Award for music.

Fisk University, also in Nashville, has a renowned chorus known as the Fisk Jubilee Singers. The school was established after the Civil War, in 1866, for the education of blacks. During the 1870s, the Fisk Jubilee Singers toured the United States and Europe and raised enough money to build the first permanent building on the campus, which was named Jubilee Hall.

All of the major cities in Tennessee have symphony orchestras, and those in Memphis and Nashville are well known. Memphis also has an operatic company—Opera Memphis.

SPORTS

Tennessee does not have any major-league sports teams. Knoxville, Chattanooga, Nashville, and Memphis, however, all have minor-league baseball teams. High-school and college baseball, basketball, and football games are well attended throughout the state.

White-water rafting on the Ocoee River

The Nashville Motor Speedway hosts stock-car races from May to October. In October, the All-American 400 pits the best drivers from the North against the best drivers from the South.

Three times a year, Memphis hosts major sports competitions. Each February, the National Indoor Tennis Tournament is held there. During the summer, the city is the site of the Danny Thomas Memphis Golf Classic. In December, football fans enjoy the Liberty Bowl Football Classic, a leading post-season, invitational bowl game.

Recreational sports such as golf, tennis, swimming, and hiking are popular everywhere in Tennessee. The many lakes, most of which are TVA reservoirs, provide facilities for swimming, boating, fishing, horseback riding, hiking, and camping. Tennessee also offers canoeing, white-water rafting, and float trips on the Buffalo, Duck, Elk, Harpeth, and Nolichucky rivers.

Within the state's borders are parts of two national parks—Great Smoky Mountains and Cumberland Gap—as well as the 604,000-acre (244,433-hectare) Cherokee National Forest. These, plus the numerous state parks and forests, provide year-round camping, hiking, and other recreational activities for Tennesseans and visitors alike.

Chapter 9

TOURING THE VOLUNTEER STATE

TOURING THE VOLUNTEER STATE

Lofty blue-hued mountains, calm lakes and rushing rivers, mysterious caves, forests, and green pastures—all these beauties existed in Tennessee long before people arrived and began to shape the land to their own needs. The region is endowed with magnificent natural assets. These alone are enough to bring hundreds of thousands of visitors to Tennessee in every season, to enjoy the scenery and to get "back to nature" for a while.

Just as impressive are the creations of people—the gigantic dams, the exciting cities, the entertainment centers, the historic sites. These, too, make a visit to the Volunteer State a special treat. Before starting the tour, let's take a look at Tennessee's mountains and lakes.

THE GREAT SMOKY MOUNTAINS

Great Smoky Mountains National Park, which runs for 70 miles (113 kilometers) on both sides of the Tennessee-North Carolina border, is the most visited of all the national parks. Its 500,000 acres (202,345 hectares) include remote wilderness, rugged hiking trails, deep forests teeming with wildlife, and some 600 miles (966 kilometers) of streams.

Cherokee Indians lived in and loved this land long before the Europeans arrived. One of the names they called the mountains meant "the place of the blue smoke" because they are nearly always covered with a blue-gray haze that looks like smoke.

The Carter Shields cabin in Cades Cove

The park is within a day's drive of most of the population centers of the eastern United States. City people crowd the highways and trails each spring to enjoy the views of hillsides ablaze with the fiery colors of azaleas and the purples, pinks, and whites of rhododendrons. Guided walks are conducted by botanists each April when the wildflowers are at their best.

About fifty kinds of animals and more than two hundred kinds of birds make their home in the Smokies. Raccoons, opossums, red foxes, white-tailed deer, and black bears are abundant.

There are two visitor centers on the Tennessee side of the park, one at Sugarlands, near Gatlinburg, and one at Cades Cove, near Townsend. Cades Cove is a mountain community with log cabins, barns, and a gristmill. Park naturalists conduct campfire programs there during the summer.

Among the attractions at the huge recreation area called Land Between the Lakes are buffalo (above) and Homeplace 1850, a living-history farm (left).

THE TVA LAKES

The Tennessee Valley Authority created most of the lakes that dot the map of Tennessee by building dams for flood control along the Tennessee River and its tributaries. These lakes have given the state hundreds of acres of recreational waters for swimming, boating, fishing, and other water sports. Many lakeside recreation areas have hotels, horseback riding and hiking trails, and facilities for picnicking and camping.

On the Kentucky-Tennessee border is a 40-mile (64-kilometer) peninsula created by the TVA called the Land Between the Lakes. This huge vacation area between Kentucky Lake and Lake Barkley stretches across the state's boundary and is shared by Tennessee and Kentucky. Facilities and attractions include a living-history farm called Homeplace 1850, campgrounds, a nature center, an environmental-education center, a buffalo herd, and facilities for hiking, biking, bird-watching, and a variety of water sports.

The Incline Railway, which takes visitors on a scenic tour up the side of Lookout Mountain, is the steepest passenger incline in the world.

Visitors are also welcome to tour the TVA dams and steam plants. Some of the major dams, and lakes that are named after them, are Boone, Cherokee, Chickamauga, Douglas, Fort Loudoun, Kentucky, Melton Hill, Normandy, Norris, Pickwick Landing, Tims Ford, and Watauga.

SOUTHEAST TENNESSEE

There are so many things to see and do in East Tennessee that visitors should divide their time between the southeast and the northeast. Both are mountainous and full of natural beauty, both were settled early and have many interesting historic sites, and both have many opportunities for outdoor recreation.

Chattanooga, southeast Tennessee's largest metropolis, is a mountainous city. If you are driving through the city, you may find that your route takes you through tunnels under the mountains. A favorite activity for visitors here is to ride the Incline Railway up the side of Lookout Mountain. It is the steepest passenger incline railroad in the world. The round trip, in glass-

This view of Chattanooga and the Tennessee River's Moccasin Bend was taken from Point Park on Lookout Mountain, where the Battle above the Clouds was fought.

roofed trains, takes about half an hour. An observation deck at the top of the mountain gives passengers some great views of the valleys below.

A Civil War battle called the Battle above the Clouds was fought on the top of Lookout Mountain. Interpretive audiovisual programs and exhibits tell the story of the battle at the visitor center of the Chickamauga-Chattanooga National Military Park at Point Park. Views of the city and of Moccasin Bend, the bend that the Tennessee River makes in Chattanooga, can be seen from an observatory in Point Park.

Also on top of the mountain is Rock City Gardens. Paths lead through beautiful gardens and rock formations. Views of seven states can be seen from a lookout point called Lovers' Leap.

Under the mountain are twin caves, called the Lookout Mountain Caverns. Ruby Falls, within the caverns, is a waterfall 145 feet (44 meters) high.

At the foot of Lookout Mountain is Confederama, a huge, three-dimensional automated display of more than five thousand miniature soldiers. The Civil War Battle of Chattanooga is recorded, complete with the lights and sounds of battle.

A popular song about this city is "The Chattanooga Choo-Choo." Two local attractions memorialize the time when the city was an important passenger-railroad hub. The Chattanooga Choo-Choo Complex is an area of shops, gardens, and restaurants where people can take rides in antique trolley cars or stay overnight in hotel rooms created in old railroad sleeping cars. The original Chattanooga Choo-Choo is displayed here.

There are several fine museums in Chattanooga. Working steam trains are on display at the Tennessee Valley Railroad Museum. Passengers can purchase rides on some of the trains. A museum that is quite unusual and a lot of fun to visit is the TVA Energy Center. Talking robots and computer games are used to tell about the world of energy.

Near Cleveland, northeast of Chattanooga, is Red Clay State Historical Area. This was the last capital of the Cherokee Nation before the infamous removal of Native Americans along the Trail of Tears. Within the park are replicas of Cherokee structures of the 1830s, hiking trails, picnic facilities, and a museum.

About halfway between Chattanooga and Knoxville, at Sweetwater, are the Lost Sea Caverns, where visitors can see what the *Guinness Book of World Records* calls the "world's largest underground lake." Taking a boat ride across this absolutely still, eerie stretch of water in the cave is a fascinating experience.

East of Sweetwater, in the village of Vonore, is the Sequoyah Birthplace Museum, near the site where the great Cherokee leader and educator was born. It is owned and operated by the Cherokee Nation. Audiovisual displays and recordings, stained-glass exhibits, and displays of historic and prehistoric artifacts help tell the story. Authentic Cherokee crafts are sold in the gift shop.

Less than 1 mile (1.6 kilometers) south of Vonore is the Fort Loudoun State Historic Area, where there is a reconstruction of the first English fort built west of the mountains. A visit to both of these sites gives one a picture of the early encounters between the Native Americans and the white settlers who eventually forced them to move away from their homelands.

NORTHEAST TENNESSEE

Knoxville is the major population center of the northeastern part of the state, and a gateway to the Great Smoky Mountains. It is the headquarters for the Tennessee Valley Authority, a manufacturing center, and the home of the Knoxville campus of the University of Tennessee.

Knoxville was the first capital of the Territory South of the River Ohio, the first capital of the state of Tennessee, and the first planned city west of the mountains. The city was planned by its founder, James White, to be a community of sixty-four lots, situated on sixteen blocks. Blount Mansion, home of William Blount, the first governor of the territory, was within this planned city. The mansion has been restored to its appearance of the late 1700s and furnished with pieces from that period.

Nearby is General James White's Fort, the original home of Knoxville's pioneer founder. Civil War history is commemorated in Confederate Memorial Hall, a fifteen-room mansion that was used by Confederate General James Longstreet as his military headquarters during the siege of Knoxville.

A few miles west of Knoxville is the city of Oak Ridge, the "secret city" built during World War II. The American Museum of

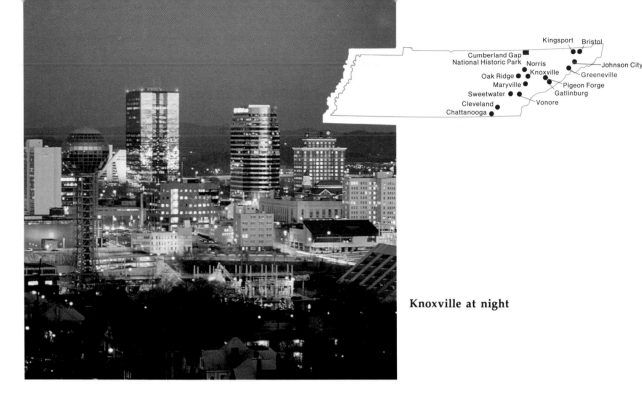

Knoxville at night

Science and Energy located there has many unusual and educational displays relating to energy, as well as a film that tells the history of the town of Oak Ridge.

Northwest of Knoxville, in Norris, is one of the finest outdoor living-history museums in the United States—the Museum of Appalachia. A former local teacher and administrator named John Rice Irwin has gathered together thousands of tools, furnishings, and entire buildings with which he has re-created a mountain village. Almost single-handedly, Irwin has managed to preserve and document a vast collection of items to illustrate a mountain way of life that is fast disappearing. Norris Dam, the first one built by the Tennessee Valley Authority, is just outside the town.

South of Knoxville, near Maryville, is a reconstructed log schoolhouse where Sam Houston once taught. A story is told that during the restoration process, construction workers found some lead knuckles with the name "Sam Houston" carved on them. They are on display in the visitor center museum. Teaching must have been a rough profession in those days!

Attractions at Pigeon Forge include the Old Mill (left) and Dolly Parton's theme park, Dollywood (above).

Southeast of Knoxville is a major route into the Great Smoky Mountains National Park, leading through the towns of Pigeon Forge and Gatlinburg. Pigeon Forge has been made famous by singing star Dolly Parton and her Heritage Home theme park, Dollywood. Lively amusement-park rides, displays of memorabilia of Dolly's life and career, shops selling authentic mountain crafts, and live shows are on view there from late April to early November. Big-name artists are featured in the shows and a national crafts festival is held during October. Comedy, country music, and gospel songs are featured at other spots in Pigeon Forge.

Both Pigeon Forge and Gatlinburg, the town just outside the national park, are crowded with every kind of tourist attraction. Wax museums, water parks, souvenir shops, motels, and sightseeing tours compete for the visitor's attention. Visitors may

This reconstruction of the cabin in which Davy Crockett was born can be seen at the Davy Crockett Birthplace State Park, near Limestone.

also view the work of many talented local artists and craftspeople at studios and galleries in Gatlinburg.

Greeneville, northeast of Gatlinburg, was the home of Andrew Johnson, the seventeenth president of the United States. His home, the tailor shop where he worked, and his grave are all preserved within the Andrew Johnson National Historic Site.

A few miles east of Greeneville, at Limestone, is Davy Crockett Birthplace State Park. A replica of his cabin, a museum of Crockett memorabilia, and a large recreational park are included.

This part of Tennessee has some fast-flowing rivers. Guided white-water raft trips on the Nolichucky and other rivers can be arranged in the nearby town of Erwin.

Jonesborough is Tennessee's oldest town. Its historic district has been restored. The Jonesborough History Museum, located in the visitor's center, is the place to start in order to learn about the

Wilbur Lake, near Elizabethton

town. Jonesborough is the headquarters of the National Association for the Advancement and Preservation of Storytelling. The annual storytelling festival held here each fall attracts participants and spectators from all over the nation and the world.

Elizabethton, just east of Jonesborough, is the site of the founding of the Watauga Association, in 1772. A mile and a half (2.4 kilometers) from town is a reconstruction of Fort Watauga at a place called Sycamore Shoals. The first settlers stopped here when they came across the Blue Ridge Mountains. Sycamore Shoals was also the gathering place for the overmountain men before they headed for Kings Mountain. A reenactment of the overmountain march to Kings Mountain, South Carolina, where a significant battle of the American Revolution took place, is held each year. An outdoor drama depicting the gathering is held each July.

The cities of Bristol, Kingsport, and Johnson City are known as Tennessee's Tri-Cities. Half of Bristol is in Tennessee and half is in Virginia. The state line runs down the center of State Street.

Four miles (6.4 kilometers) northeast of Johnson City is Rocky Mount Historic Site and Overmountain Museum. Territorial Governor William Blount lived here in a two-and-half-story log cabin. The house served as the territorial capital from 1790 to 1792. It has been restored, and costumed interpreters act out the parts of people who might have lived and worked there in the late 1700s. Outbuildings include a kitchen, a slave cabin, a barn, a smokehouse, and a blacksmith shop.

South of Johnson City, at the Tipton-Haynes Historical Farm, exhibits in several original buildings and reconstructions illustrate four periods of history: colonial, Revolutionary War, War of 1812, and Civil War.

Kingsport is the principal city of the northeastern triangle of Tennessee. It, too, was an early settlement. A trail that later became part of Daniel Boone's historic Wilderness Road came through here in 1761. The Kingsport Press, one of the largest producers of books in the world, is located here.

The Netherlands Inn, now a museum, was a stop on the Great Stage Road. Two presidents, Jackson and Johnson, stopped here during its 150-year history as an inn.

Bays Mountain Park is an outstanding nature center and one of the largest city parks in the nation. There are 25 miles (40 kilometers) of trails, a small zoo, a planetarium, and much more. Barge trips on the 44-acre (18-hectare) lake often cruise close to beaver lodges.

Cumberland Gap National Historic Park, covering more than 20,000 acres (8,094 hectares) at the place where Tennessee, Kentucky, and Virginia meet, commemorates the blazing of a trail

A view from the Pinnacle Overlook at Cumberland Gap

into the wilderness by Daniel Boone and his band of scouts. There are campgrounds; trails; a visitor center; the Pinnacle, from which visitors can see parts of the surrounding states; and Civil War cannons left from the Union and Confederate fortifications.

Lincoln Memorial University, in nearby Harrogate, has an outstanding museum of Abraham Lincoln and Civil War materials. There are many museums of Lincolniana, but this collection is one of the largest anywhere, comprising more than 250,000 items.

MIDDLE TENNESSEE

Just as the Volunteer State is called the three states of Tennessee, one might describe its capital city as the "several cities of Nashville." It is a government city, with graceful state buildings

Nashville, on the Cumberland River

housing administrative offices, the general assembly, the state
library, and a fine state museum and cultural center. It is a
financial city, home to numerous banks, investment firms, and
insurance companies. It is a printing and publishing city, issuing
Bibles, sheet music, materials for religious education, and more. It
is a cultural and educational city, proud of its universities, its
museums, and its traditional nickname, Athens of the South. It is
Music City, USA, headquarters of a huge musical entertainment
industry. And it is an important tourist city.

The radio show Grand Ole Opry, performed on stage before a
live audience for more than sixty years, started it all. Visitors
began flocking to Nashville to watch the Grand Old Opry long
before there were any other tourist attractions. The Opry performs
several times a week during the height of the tourist season. The
Grand Old Opry is now a part of Opryland USA, a complex that
also includes the Opryland theme park, the *General Jackson*
showboat, the Acuff Theatre, and The Nashville Network studios.

The "several cities" of Nashville have a great variety of things
to see and do. The Tennessee State Museum, housed in the

A full-size replica of the Parthenon stands in Nashville's Centennial Park.

James K. Polk State Building, has exhibits on life in the region from 12,000 B.C. through A.D. 1920.

The Hermitage, President Andrew Jackson's home, is a beautiful classical mansion on a huge estate with gardens and outbuildings. Visitors discover what life was like for successful farmers of that period.

Cheekwood is an estate that includes the Tennessee Fine Arts Center, with a collection of nineteenth- and twentieth-century American art; and the Tennessee Botanical Gardens, which include formal plantings, a Japanese garden, a public greenhouse, and beds of herbs, roses, and wildflowers.

In Centennial Park, which was built to honor the state's one hundredth birthday, in 1897, is a full-sized replica of the Parthenon in Athens, Greece. It houses fine paintings and reproductions of the Elgin marbles.

The Country Music Hall of Fame and Museum has a varied collection of items that belonged to various country music stars. A research library is housed in the basement. The Cumberland Museum and Science Center has natural-history exhibits and live animals. Laser light displays are shown in the museum's planetarium. Many other museums in and near Nashville include mansions, car collections, wax museums, a toy museum, and a museum of religious art. Several personal museums belonging to country music stars are also open to the public.

The Natchez Trace Parkway is a gently winding highway administered by the National Park Service. Its 444-mile (715-kilometer) route leads in a southwesterly direction from Nashville through Tennessee and Alabama to Natchez, Mississippi. The trace was a historic foot and horse trail used by Native Americans, buffalo herds, settlers, soldiers, circuit-riding preachers, and highwaymen. Today, it provides a scenic and leisurely drive past tidy farms and through wilderness areas, plus an opportunity to pause along the way and learn a bit about the region's early history.

Southeast of Nashville, near Murfreesboro, is Stones River National Battlefield and Cemetery. The battle commemorated here was especially fierce, resulting in 10,000 casualties among Confederate troops and 13,000 among the Union forces. The battle opened the way for Union armies to advance to Chattanooga. There are 6,900 graves in the national cemetery. Also in Murfreesboro is nineteenth-century Oaklands Mansion museum. It was built in three stages between 1815 and 1850. Cannonsburgh Pioneer Village is a reconstruction of an early nineteenth-century settlement, complete with a working blacksmith shop.

South of Nashville is Columbia, where James K. Polk, the eleventh president of the United States, spent his boyhood. He

Oaklands Mansion, in Murfreesboro, was built in three stages between 1815 and 1850.

also opened his first law office here. Polk's boyhood home here is furnished with items used by his family.

Farther to the southwest, on the Tennessee River near the Mississippi border, is Shiloh National Military Park. Shiloh was one of the bitterest and bloodiest battles in all military history. Nearly 24,000 men on both sides were killed, wounded, or missing in the two-day fray. Two-thirds of the 3,800 soldiers buried here were never identified. In addition to the battlefield, there is a Civil War library and exhibits of relics and maps in the visitor center.

WEST TENNESSEE

Reelfoot Lake, in the northwest corner of the state, was created by a severe earthquake in 1811-12. Today it is a fisher's paradise, with more than fifty-six species, including trout, living in the

Memphis, on the Mississippi River

shallow waters. Most of the area around the lake is a nature preserve, where bird-watchers have counted more than 240 species. Reelfoot Lake Resort Park has an inn, a restaurant, and a landing strip for small planes. This is the primary outdoor recreation area in West Tennessee.

Just off Interstate 40, between Memphis and Nashville, is the little town of Jackson. It was the home of a railroading man made very famous in song. Nearly every American has heard "The Ballad of Casey Jones." Jones was a railroad engineer who tried, unsuccessfully, to stop his train in time to avoid a collision with another train that had stalled on the tracks. He could have jumped to safety, but he didn't, and he was the only casualty of the wreck. Casey Jones's home in Jackson is now a historic site and museum.

Memphis, on the Mississippi River, is the largest city in all the southeastern states. It is an exciting city to visit, full of restored historic areas, museums, and other interesting places to see.

Memphis has been, and still is, an important commercial city. In the last century, its wealth came from cotton trading and shipping. Today, the industries and businesses are diversified and include the manufacture of furniture and structural steel.

The city's front door is the Mississippi River. A city theme park, Mud Island, pays tribute to the river's importance to Memphis and the south-central United States. Visitors may walk the five-block-long replica of the river from Cairo, Illinois, to the Gulf of Mexico. The Mississippi River Museum and an amphitheater that hosts popular entertainers are also on the island.

Beale Street, home of the distinctive Memphis sound of the blues, has been restored and is an entertainment center. The city's black history is remembered at places such as W. C. Handy Park. Beale Street music festivals are held in May and September.

Chucalissa Indian Village and Museum is the site of a Native American village that flourished on the bluffs of the Mississippi River for about six centuries. Archaeologists from Memphis State University have uncovered and reconstructed native houses and a temple.

Also in Memphis is Elvis Presley's home, Graceland. The home and his private plane are open for public tours, and his huge collection of fancy cars is on display. Among the city's other outstanding attractions are the Brooks Museum of Art and the Memphis Botanic Gardens. The Pink Palace Museum and Planetarium was given to the city by the founder of the Piggly Wiggly supermarket chain. It has exhibits on the natural and cultural history of the area.

No visitor to Memphis should miss the twice-daily Parade of the Ducks at the Peabody Hotel. Crowds come to the hotel to watch these ducks, who spend their days in the hotel's lobby fountain and their nights in a penthouse home on the hotel roof.

Elvis Presley's mansion, Graceland (left), and Hebe Fountain, in Court Square (right), are among the sights to be seen in Memphis.

Their entrances to and exits from the fountain are popular events. They march across a red carpet to the accompaniment of band music, and people crowd around to watch them.

From Davy Crockett to Elvis Presley, from Andrew Jackson to Dolly Parton, Tennessee has produced scores of independent, individualistic, colorful citizens. And the people of the state honor them all. A tourist who visits the state and listens to its people soon realizes that the Volunteer State has played a large part in shaping the character of the nation.

FACTS AT A GLANCE

GENERAL INFORMATION

Statehood: June 1, 1796, sixteenth state

Origin of Name: The name was probably adapted from the name of the principal Cherokee village, Tenasie

State Capital: Nashville, settled in 1780, incorporated in 1784

State Nickname: "Volunteer State," originated during the War of 1812, in which volunteer soldiers from Tennessee displayed marked valor in the Battle of New Orleans. Tennessee has also been called the "Big Bend State," for the bend in the Tennessee River; and at one time the "Hog and Hominy State," for its agricultural products.

State Flag: A blue circular field with a border of white is in the center of a red flag. Three five-pointed stars in the field represent the state's three general divisions—East, Middle, and West Tennessee. On the free, or fly, side of the flag is a blue bar separated from the red flag by a narrow band of white.

State Motto: Agriculture and Commerce

State Slogan: "Tennessee—America at its Best"

State Bird: Mockingbird

State Wild Animal: Raccoon

State Wildflower: Passionflower

State Cultivated Flower: Iris

State Tree: Tulip poplar

State Insects: Firefly and ladybug

State Gem: Freshwater pearl

State Rocks: Limestone and agate

State Songs: Tennessee's legislature has adopted five official songs. The first, "My Homeland, Tennessee" (words by Nell Grayson Taylor, music by Roy Lamont Smith), was adopted in 1925. The second, "When It's Iris Time in Tennessee" (words and music by Willa Waid Newman), was adopted in 1935. In 1955, "My Tennessee," by Frances Hannah Tranum, was adopted as the official state public school song. "Tennessee Waltz" (words by Pee Wee King and music by Redd Stewart) became Tennessee's fourth official song in 1965. "Rocky Top," by Boudleaux and Felice Bryant, was adopted as an official state song in 1982.

My Homeland, Tennessee

O Tennessee, that gave us birth
To thee our hearts bow down.
For thee our love and loyalty
Shall weave a fadeless crown.
Thy purple hills our cradle was,
Thy fields our mother breast.
Beneath thy sunny bended skies,
Our childhood days were blessed.

'Twas long ago our fathers came,
A free and noble band,
Across the mountain's frowning heights
To seek a promised land.
And here before their raptured eyes;
In beauteous majesty:
Outspread the smiling valleys
Of the winding Tennessee.

Could we forget our heritage
Of heroes strong and brave?
Could we do aught but cherish it,
Unsullied to the grave?
Ah no! the State where Jackson sleeps
Shall ever peerless be.
We glory in thy majesty;
Our homeland, Tennessee.

Chorus:

O Tennessee: Fair Tennessee:
Our love for thee can never die;
Dear homeland, Tennessee.

When It's Iris Time in Tennessee

Sweetness of Spring memories bring
Of a place I long to be.
Land of Sunshine calls this old heart of Mine,
Come back to Tennessee.

Rocks and the rills deep tinted hills,
There's no spot so dear to me.
Where'er I roam still it's my Home Sweet Home,
My own, my Tennessee.

Chorus:

When it's Iris time down in Tennessee,
I'll be coming back to stay
Where the mockingbird sings at the break of day
A lilting love song gay.
Where the Iris grows,
Where the Harpeth flows,
That is where I long to be.
There's a picture there that lives in memory
When it's Iris time in Tennessee.

Rocky Top

Wish that I was on ol' Rocky Top,
    down in the Tennessee hills;
Ain't no smoggy smoke on Rocky Top;
Ain't no telephone bills;
Once I had a girl on Rocky Top;
Half bear, other half cat;
Wild as a mink, but sweet as soda pop,
    I still dream about that;

Once two strangers climbed ol' Rocky Top
    lookin' for a moonshine still;
Strangers ain't come down from Rocky Top;
Reckon they never will;
Corn won't grow at all on Rocky Top;
Dirt's too rocky by far;
That's why all the folks on Rocky Top
    get their corn from a jar.

I've had years of cramped-up city life
    Trapped like a duck in a pen;
All I know is it's a pity life
Can't be simple again.

Chorus:

Rocky Top, you'll always be
home sweet home to me;
Good ol' Rocky Top;
Rocky Top, Tennessee;
Rocky Top, Tennessee.

My Tennessee

Beloved state, oh state of mine,
In all the world I could not find,
Where God has strewn with lavish hand,
More natural beauty o'er the land.
From ev'ry stream and valley green
His wond'rous art is ever seen.
Ah, let my heart beat true to thee,
And swell with pride for Tennessee.

Thy rocks and rills, and wooded hills,
My mem'ry keeps the childhood thrills
You gave to me, that I might know
The joys supreme, you could bestow.
The song of birds, the whisp'ring trees,
The low of herds, the hum of bees,
It all comes back so dear to me,
My childhood home in Tennessee.

Your battles fought, and vict'ries won,
Your freedom bought and duty done.
With daughters fair, and sons so brave,
To do and dare, their deeds they gave.
Courageously, without a fear,
And won the name of volunteer.
In sacred trust, let those who will,
By being just, preserve it still.

Chorus:

Oh, Tennessee, My Tennessee,
Thy hills and vales are fair to see,
With mountains grand, and fertile lands
There is no state more dear to me.
Thro' other climes tho I may roam,
There will be times I'll long for home,
In Tennessee, Fair Tennessee,
The land of my nativity.

Tennessee Waltz

I was waltzing with my darlin' to the *Tennessee Waltz*
When an old friend I happened to see
Introduced him to my loved one and while they were waltzing
My friend stole my sweetheart from me.

I remember the night and the *Tennessee Waltz*
Now I know just how much I have lost
Yes I lost my little darlin' the night they were playing
The beautiful *Tennessee Waltz*.

POPULATION

Population: 4,591,120, seventeenth among the states (1980 census)

Population Density: 109 people per sq. mi. (42 people per km²)

Population Distribution: In 1960, for the first time in the state's history, more people were living in cities and towns than on farms and in rural areas. According to the 1980 census, 60 percent of all Tennesseans lived in towns and cities of 2,500 or more; 36 percent lived in towns with more than 25,000; 35 percent lived in the twelve largest cities.

Memphis	646,174
Nashville	455,651
Knoxville	175,045
Chattanooga	169,728
Clarksville	54,777
Jackson	49,131
Johnson City	39,753
Murfreesboro	32,845
Kingsport	32,027
Oak Ridge	27,662
Columbia	26,571

(Population figures according to 1980 census)

Population Growth:

Year	Population
1790	35,691
1800	105,602
1810	261,727
1820	422,823
1830	681,904
1840	829,210
1850	1,002,717
1860	1,109,801
1870	1,258,520
1880	1,542,359
1890	1,767,518
1900	2,020,616
1910	2,184,789
1920	2,337,885
1930	2,616,556
1940	2,915,841
1950	3,291,718
1960	3,567,089
1970	3,926,018
1980	4,591,120

GEOGRAPHY

Borders: Tennessee is bounded on the east by North Carolina, on the north by Virginia and Kentucky, on the west by Missouri and Arkansas across the Mississippi River, and on the south by Mississippi, Alabama, and Georgia.

Highest Point: Clingmans Dome, 6,643 ft. (2,025 m) above sea level

Lowest Point: In Shelby County, on the Mississippi River, 182 ft. (55 m) above sea level

Greatest Distances: East to west—430 mi. (692 km)
North to south—110 mi. (177 km)

Area: 42,114 sq. mi. (109,075 km²)

Rank in Area Among the States: Thirty-fourth

Rivers: Tennessee has three river systems: the Mississippi River, which forms the western boundary of the state; the Tennessee River, which cuts through the state in the eastern part, then loops south and comes back into Tennessee in the western part; and the Cumberland River, in the north-central section. Several tributaries feed these three main rivers.

Lakes: Tennessee has few natural lakes of any size; the largest is Reelfoot, in northwestern Tennessee. However, many artificial lakes have been formed by dams on the Tennessee and Cumberland rivers. The dams were constructed to provide flood control, hydroelectric energy, and soil and water conservation. The lakes and surrounding areas are also popular for recreation. Some of the major lakes are Barkley, Center Hill, Cherokee, Chickamauga, Dale Hollow, Douglas, J. Priest, Kentucky, Norris, Old Hickory, Pickwick Landing, and Tims Ford.

Topography: Tennessee is divided into six topographical areas. In the Blue Ridge area, the Great Smoky Mountains make up the highest and most rugged part of the state. The Appalachian Ridge and Valley of East Tennessee is a region of long, narrow, wooded ridges with broad, fertile valleys between them. The Cumberland Plateau, a region of flat-topped mountains and V-shaped valleys, is the main coal-producing area of the state. The Highland Rim, in Middle Tennessee, is a gently rolling area encircling the Great Central (or Nashville) Basin. The basin is like the bottom of an oval dish; it is an area of rich, fertile farmland and is also the most densely populated area of the state. The Gulf Coastal Plain is a broad area that slopes toward the Mississippi River, ending abruptly at a steep bluff overlooking the river. The Mississippi Alluvial Plain, a flat strip along the river averaging less than 300 ft. (91 m) above sea level; and the Mississippi Bottoms, low, rolling hills and wide valleys, are part of the Gulf Coastal Plain.

Climate: Tennessee's climate is temperate; extremes of heat and cold are rare. The mountainous regions of the east have more snow (10 in./25 cm), shorter

Spectacular azaleas are among the wildflowers that grow in Tennessee.

growing seasons, and lower temperatures than the lowlands and plains of western Tennessee. The average temperatures in the east are 37° F. (3° C) in January and 71° F. (22° C) in July. In the west, temperatures range from 40° F. (4° C) in January to 79° F. (26° C) in July. The highest recorded temperature was 113° F. (45° C) at Perryville, on August 9, 1930. The lowest was -32° F. (-36° C) at Mountain City, on December 30, 1917. Average precipitation is 52 in. (132 cm) a year.

NATURE

Trees: Tulip poplars, shortleaf pines, chestnuts, black and red oaks, hickories, ashes, pines, gum maples, black walnuts, sycamores, cottonwoods, cypresses

Wild Plants: Rhododendrons, mountain laurels, azaleas, passionflowers, irises, dragonroots, dwarf evening primroses, hop clover, spring beauties, yellow jasmines

Animals: Raccoons, white-tailed deer, black bears, bobcats, muskrats, woodchucks, opossums, red and gray foxes, European wild boars

Birds: Bobwhites, mourning doves, sparrows, pied-billed grebes, wood ducks, killdeer, red-tailed hawks, woodpeckers, owls, crows, blue jays, Carolina chickadees, tufted titmice, white-breasted nuthatches, wrens, robins, eastern bluebirds, northern mockingbirds, red-winged blackbirds, cardinals, goldfinches

Fish: Catfish, bream, bass, crappie, pike, trout

GOVERNMENT

Tennessee has three branches of government—executive, judicial, and legislative. The executive branch is run by the elected governor and the governor's appointees. The governor is elected to a four-year term and may be reelected for a second term. The executive branch is responsible for the enforcement of the laws, the collection of taxes, and the general well-being of the state and its citizens. According to the state constitution, the governor must be at least thirty years of age, a citizen of the United States, and a citizen of Tennessee for the seven years preceding election.

The legislative department of the state is the General Assembly, which consists of a senate and a house of representatives. There are ninety-nine representatives and thirty-three senators. Senators are elected to four-year terms, and there is no limit to the number of terms a senator may serve. Those from even-numbered districts are elected in one general election, and those representing the odd-numbered districts are elected two years later.

Representatives are elected to two-year terms with all the representatives standing for election at the same time. There is no limit on the number of terms a representative may serve.

The General Assembly meets in Nashville on the second Tuesday in January of each odd-numbered year. The organizational session, during which various officers of each house are elected, may take up to fifteen consecutive calendar days. After the organizational session, the General Assembly is required to begin its legislative session the following Tuesday and is limited to ninety legislative days over a two-year period. The Assembly may be called into Extraordinary Session by the governor or by the speakers of the two houses at the request of two-thirds of the members of each house.

The power of the judicial branch is vested in a supreme court and a system of other courts established by the legislature. The supreme court consists of five judges who are elected by the voters of the state for an eight-year term. The attorney general and reporter for the state are appointed by the judges of the supreme court.

The judicial branch interprets the laws, tries cases, and serves as a check on the powers of both the legislative and executive branches of the state government. There are four levels of courts—the supreme court, composed of five justices popularly elected to eight-year terms; the intermediate appellate courts, such as the court of appeals and court of criminal appeals; the general trial courts, such as the chancery, criminal, and circuit courts; and the municipal, probate, general sessions, and juvenile courts.

Number of Counties: 95

U.S. Representatives: 9

Electoral Votes: 11

Voting Qualifications: Eighteen years of age, citizen of the United States, registered to vote at least thirty days before the election

EDUCATION

Tennessee has 140 public school districts, serving approximately 850,000 students. Free public education, including kindergarten, is available for all persons between six and twenty-one years of age. Children between the ages of seven and sixteen must attend school. A ten-member state board of education, appointed by the governor, is the governing and policy-making body for the state's public elementary and secondary schools. Nearly half of the tax money collected by the state is used for education.

Approximately 54 percent of all students in grades seven through twelve attend vocational education programs. About one hundred different occupations are covered in these schools. Five special state schools serve the needs of deaf, blind, dependent, and neglected children.

State facilities for higher education include the University of Tennessee, with campuses in Knoxville, Chattanooga, Martin, and Memphis; state universities in Clarksville, Johnson City, Memphis, Murfreesboro, and Nashville; and ten two-year community colleges. Well-known private colleges include Fisk University and Vanderbilt University, in Nashville; and the University of the South, in Sewanee.

ECONOMY AND INDUSTRY

Principal Products:
Agriculture: Soybeans, tobacco, cotton, corn, strawberries, vegetables, wheat, beef cattle, hogs and pigs, sheep and lambs, dairy cattle, poultry and eggs, horses

Manufacturing: Clothing and textiles, lumber and furniture, chemicals and allied products, dairy products and processed foods, metal and metal products, electrical and electronic equipment, nonelectrical machinery, transportation equipment

Mining: Copper, zinc, iron, lead, manganese, gold, coal, clay, portland cement, sand, gravel, stone

Communication: Memphis has the newspaper with the largest circulation in the state—the *Commercial Appeal*—followed by Nashville's *Tennessean.* Ten morning newspapers, 22 evening dailies, and 15 Sunday newspapers are published in Tennessee. There are 278 radio stations and 29 television stations.

Transportation: Tennessee's road system stretches 84,351 mi. (135,746 km), of which 13,457 mi. (21,656 km) are major highways that include 1,062 mi. (1,709 km) of the interstate expressways. Interstates 40 and 81 cross the state from east to west; Interstates 24, 65, and 75, from north to south.

There are approximately 1,000 mi. (1,609 km) of navigable waterways in Tennessee. The entire length of the Tennessee River is navigable. The newest addition to this system is the Tennessee-Tombigbee Waterway, which gives vessels direct north-south passage between the Tennessee River and the Gulf of Mexico.

Today, Tennessee has 2,785 mi. (4,482 km) of Class 1 railroad track. The only passenger train going through the state serves Memphis on the route between Chicago and New Orleans. The main business of the railroad transportation system at present is hauling freight.

Air transportation is important to Tennessee. There are more than 130 private and public airports. Memphis International Airport is the largest and busiest. Chattanooga, Nashville, and Knoxville are also important hubs for air traffic.

SOCIAL AND CULTURAL LIFE

Museums: The Tennessee State Museum is located in two buildings in downtown Nashville—the James K. Polk State Office Building and the War Memorial Building. Various exhibits present Tennessee history from prehistoric times to the present. Of special interest are a full-scale gristmill, a workable reproduction of a 1700s printing press, and artifacts belonging to famous Tennesseans.

A living-history museum, the Museum of Appalachia, in Norris, is a reconstructed mountain village and a 70-acre (28-hectare) working farm. Cades Cove, in the Great Smoky Mountains, is another outdoor museum reflecting the life of mountain people.

More than 23,000 volumes dealing with the history and genealogy of Tennessee and the southeastern United States are housed in the East Tennessee Historical Center, in Knoxville. Also in Knoxville is the Confederate Memorial Hall, a restored fifteen-room antebellum mansion that served as Confederate headquarters during the siege of Knoxville. The Mississippi River Museum, on Mud Island in Memphis, traces the development of life, transportation, technology, and music along the Mississippi.

The American Museum of Science and Energy, in Oak Ridge, has one of the world's largest energy exhibits. Among its features are hands-on experiments, a slide show, movies, and varied demonstrations. The Cumberland Science Museum, in Nashville, features a planetarium.

Art museums and galleries can be found throughout the state. Some of the most noted are the Dixon Gallery and Gardens and the Brooks Memorial Art Gallery, in Memphis; the Hunter Museum of Art and the Houston Antique Museum, both in Chattanooga; the Dulin Gallery, in Knoxville; and the Tennessee Botanical Gardens and Fine Arts Center, in Nashville.

Special-interest museums include the National Knife Museum, in Chattanooga; the Tennessee Valley Railroad Museum, also in Chattanooga, where a steam-powered passenger train travels 6 mi. (10 km) over three bridges and through a railroad tunnel; Casey Jones Home and Railroad Museum, near Jackson; and the Museum of Tobacco Art and History, in Nashville. The Country Music Hall of Fame and Museum, Country Music Wax Museum, Jim Reeves Museum, and Minnie Pearl's Museum, all in Nashville, highlight various country music stars and their work. The Graceland complex, in Memphis, includes Elvis Presley's home, two airplanes, a touring bus, a car collection, all his gold and platinum records, and other memorabilia.

Libraries: Libraries were founded in the very early years of Tennessee's history. The first one was in Charlotte, in 1811. The Nashville Library Company, founded in 1813, was the state's first public library.

The State Library in Nashville owes its beginning to Andrew Johnson. When he was governor of the state, in 1854, he asked the legislature for an appropriation of

$5,000 to start a state library. Today, that institution has more than a quarter of a million volumes, including many records and materials about the state's history that cannot be found anywhere else.

There are about 250 public libraries and nearly 50 academic libraries in the state, with a total of well over six million books. The largest university collections in the state are in the libraries at Vanderbilt University, Memphis State University, the University of Tennessee at Knoxville, and East Tennessee State University at Johnson City. Other large depositories are the Memphis-Shelby County, Knoxville-Knox County, and Chattanooga-Hamilton County libraries.

Performing Arts: The Grand Ole Opry is the premier performing attraction in the state of Tennessee. The nation's oldest continuous radio program, started in 1925, performs regularly in the 4,400-seat Grand Ole Opry House adjacent to Nashville's Opryland theme park. Other country music shows are presented there as well. Country music, gospel music, jazz, and the blues are all part of Tennessee's musical heritage. W. C. Handy created a special musical form in 1909. Known as "Memphis Blues," it is a blend of Dixieland jazz and work songs. The blues can be heard along Beale Street in Memphis every night.

The Nashville Symphony and Memphis Symphony are the best known of Tennessee's symphony orchestras, but many smaller towns also have orchestras. Memphis is also the home of Opera Memphis.

Sports and Recreation: Baseball is popular in Tennessee; Knoxville, Chattanooga, and Memphis all have minor-league teams. Basketball and football, as well as baseball, are well-attended high-school and collegiate spectator sports.

Golf, tennis, swimming, and hiking are popular throughout the state. The Great Smoky Mountains National Park, the most visited national park in the nation, attracts visitors all year round. The 604,000-acre (244,433-hectare) Cherokee National Forest offers both primitive and highly developed recreation areas, as do the numerous state parks. Many lakes, most of which are Tennessee Valley Authority reservoirs, provide facilities for water sports and recreation.

Memphis hosts the Liberty Bowl Football Classic, a leading intercollegiate football match, each December. The city is also the site of the National Indoor Tennis Tournament in February and the Danny Thomas Memphis Golf Classic in the summer.

Historic Sites and Landmarks:

Andrew Johnson National Historic Site, in Greeneville, includes the tailor shop, the homestead, and the burial place of the seventeenth president of the United States.

Beale Street, in downtown Memphis, is where W. C. Handy wrote "Memphis Blues," "St. Louis Blues," and other classic tunes.

Cannonsburgh Pioneer Village, in Murfreesboro, is a reconstruction of a southern village of the late 1800s.

Chickamauga and Chattanooga National Military Park, in Chattanooga, spreads across the Tennessee-Georgia border. This was the scene of one of the Civil War's

A table setting in the cabin at Davy Crockett Birthplace Park, near Limestone

fiercest battles, in 1863. The Tennessee area includes Point Park, on Lookout Mountain, and Signal Park, on Signal Mountain.

Chucalissa Indian Village and Museum, in Memphis, is an archaeological project of Memphis State University and the site of an Indian village founded about A.D. 900. Several village buildings have been reconstructed, and at certain times of the year, Native Americans demonstrate traditional crafts.

Cordell Hull Birthplace, in Byrdstown, is the log-cabin birthplace of the Tennessee statesman who was instrumental in the establishment of the United Nations.

Cumberland Gap National Historic Park, northwest of Cumberland Gap, covers an area in Tennessee, Kentucky, and Virginia that is both historic and beautiful. Settlers moving west followed Daniel Boone's Wilderness Road through the mountain gap.

Davy Crockett Birthplace Park, near Limestone, has a replica of the log cabin in which Crockett was born, in 1786.

Fort Donelson National Military Park and Cemetery, west of Dover, was the site of a four-day battle won by General Ulysses S. Grant in 1862. The fort's walls, outer defenses, and river batteries are part of a self-guided auto tour.

Fort Loudoun, near Vonore, is a reconstruction of a fort built by the British in 1756 and destroyed by the Cherokees in 1760. Across the Little Tennessee River from the fort is *Tellico Blockhouse,* the site of treaty negotiations with the Cherokees, later used as a trading post.

Fort Nashborough, in Nashville, is a reproduction of the log fort built in 1780 near this site.

Governor William Blount Mansion, in Knoxville, is the restored home of the governor of the Territory of the United States South of the River Ohio. It was the center of military, political, and social activities in the territory during the late 1790s.

The Hermitage, in Nashville, was the home of Andrew Jackson, seventh president of the United States. The stately house and grounds have been beautifully preserved. Jackson and his wife, Rachel, are buried in the garden. Nearby is *Tulip Grove*, the residence of Jackson's nephew Andrew Jackson Donelson.

James K. Polk's Ancestral Home, in Columbia, was built in 1816 by Samuel Polk, father of the eleventh president of the United States.

Jonesborough Historic District, in Jonesborough, reflects two hundred years of Tennessee history. The short-lived state of Franklin was formed there in 1784.

The Natchez Trace is a 444-mi. (715-km) scenic and historic parkway between Nashville, Tennessee, and Natchez, Mississippi. It was the early pathway of Native Americans, settlers, soldiers, and ministers of pioneer days. Marked sites along the way commemorate historic events.

Rhea County Courthouse, on the grounds of Bryan College in Dayton, was the scene of the 1925 Scopes trial.

Rocky Mount Historic Site and Overmountain Museum, near Johnson City, includes the restored log house that served as the territorial capitol in 1790.

Sam Davis Home, outside Smyrna, tells the story of a twenty-one-year-old Tennessean who was tried and executed as a Confederate spy during the Civil War. The two-story house is part of a 168-acre (68-hectare) working farm that is open to the public.

Sequoyah Birthplace Museum, in Vonore, honors the brilliant Cherokee chief who developed a written alphabet for the Cherokee language.

Shiloh National Military Park, southeast of Savannah, preserves the site of one of the fiercest battles of the Civil War. Two days of fighting resulted in nearly 24,000 casualties.

Tipton-Haynes Historical Farm, south of Johnson City, consists of six original buildings and four reconstructions from four periods of American history: colonial, Revolutionary War, War of 1812, and Civil War.

Other Interesting Places to Visit:

American Museum of Science and Energy, in Oak Ridge, one of the world's largest energy exhibits, has computer games, live demonstrations, and more than two hundred displays.

Belle Meade, near Nashville, was a famous Thoroughbred breeding farm. On the grounds are the Greek Revival-style mansion house, a log cabin used as a way station on the Natchez Trace, and an elaborate carriage house-stable.

Little Pigeon River in the Great Smoky Mountains National Park

Chattanooga Choo-Choo, in Chattanooga, is a 1905 train station converted into shops, a hotel, five restaurants, and an entertainment area. On the tracks are forty-eight sleeping cars now used as hotel rooms.

Childrens Museum of Oak Ridge, in Oak Ridge, has hands-on exhibits and displays of early Appalachian life, Native American life, and space travel.

Country Music Hall of Fame and Museum, in Nashville, has memorabilia of country music stars and one of Elvis Presley's Cadillacs. It also includes the recording studio where much of the music that made Nashville famous was created.

Dollywood, in Pigeon Forge, is Dolly Parton's Heritage Home theme park. Musical shows are presented and pioneer and regional crafts are demonstrated.

Forbidden Caverns, near Sevierville, were inhabited by Native Americans hundreds of years before white settlers explored the caves. There are natural chimneys, waterfalls, and underground streams.

Graceland, in Memphis, was the home of the late Elvis Presley. On display are many of his possessions, including his unbelievably large collection of gold and platinum records.

Great Smoky Mountains National Park, southeast of Knoxville, spans the border between Tennessee and North Carolina. The huge park, which includes the highest mountain range in the eastern United States, has extensive opportunities for outdoor recreation.

Children enjoy wading in the five-block-long scale model of the lower Mississippi River on Mud Island, in Memphis.

Knoxville Zoological Park, in Knoxville, has one of the largest collections of big cats in the country. Other exhibits include a Marine Mammal Center and an African Plains habitat.

Lookout Mountain, in Chattanooga, has a viewpoint where, on a clear day, visitors can see into five states (Tennessee, Georgia, North Carolina, South Carolina, and Alabama). It was the site of a Civil War skirmish called the Battle above the Clouds.

Lookout Mountain Incline, in Chattanooga, is the steepest inclined passenger railroad in the world.

Memphis Zoo and Aquarium, in Memphis's Overton Park, has a collection of more than two thousand animals.

Mud Island, in Memphis, is a city-owned park, accessible from shore by a monorail or foot bridge. Attractions include a river museum, a five-block-long scale model of the lower Mississippi River, the famous World War II B-17 aircraft *Memphis Belle*, and other exhibits related to the Mississippi River.

Norris Dam, north of Norris, was the first dam built by the Tennessee Valley Authority (TVA) for the purposes of flood control and the manufacture of electricity. Norris Dam State Park includes a museum, an eighteenth-century gristmill, a threshing barn, nature trails, and recreational facilities.

Opryland, in Nashville, is a theme park devoted primarily to American music, from gospel and country to rock and roll and musical comedy. Included at the complex are The Nashville Network cable television studios, the Grand Ole Opry House, and the *General Jackson*, a four-deck paddle-wheel show boat.

Roan Mountain State Park, in Elizabethton, is a 600-acre (243-hectare) scenic and recreational park on top of a mountain that has spectacular displays of rhododendrons in late June.

Rugby, east of Jamestown, was founded by Englishman Thomas Hughes as a Utopian experiment, in the 1880s. Seventeen of the original buildings still stand.

Tennessee Botanical Gardens and Fine Arts Center, in Nashville, is a complex that includes a collection of nineteenth- and twentieth-century American art in a stately 1932 Georgian mansion, 30 acres (12 hectares) of formal and wildflower gardens, greenhouses, and Botanic Hall, where a lavish display of Christmas trees is presented each year.

IMPORTANT DATES

1540-41—Spanish explorers under Hernando De Soto cross the region now known as Tennessee

1673—Two British explorers come into the Tennessee River Valley; Father Jacques Marquette of France and Louis Jolliet of Canada stop at Chickasaw Bluffs while exploring the Mississippi River

1682—René-Robert Cavelier, Sieur de La Salle, claims the entire Mississippi Valley for France; Fort Prud'homme, believed to be the first structure erected by Europeans in Tennessee, is built on Chickasaw Bluffs

1714—French trader Charles Charleville establishes a trading post at French Lick, where Nashville now stands

1730—Sir Alexander Cuming negotiates the first treaty between the English and the Cherokees

1739—The French build Fort Assumption at the site of present-day Memphis

1750—Dr. Thomas Walker leads an exploration party through upper East Tennessee; they discover the Cumberland Gap and pass into Kentucky

1763—France surrenders to England all claims on lands east of the Mississippi River

1769—William Bean builds a cabin on Boone's Creek and begins what is thought to be the first permanent European settlement in Tennessee

1772—The Watauga Association is established and adopts one of the first written documents of self-government in North America

1775—Richard Henderson and the Transylvania Land Company buy Cherokee land between the Kentucky and Cumberland rivers

1779—Jonesborough becomes the first town established in Tennessee

1780—Settlers in Middle Tennessee sign the Cumberland Compact, establishing representative government for all settlers and creating a court system; Tennessee troops participate in the Battle of Kings Mountain, helping to turn the tide of the Revolutionary War

1784—Three counties in East Tennessee secede from North Carolina, form the independent state of Franklin, and adopt a constitution

1787—The *Tennessee Gazette* is established as the first newspaper in Nashville

1788—The government of Franklin collapses and North Carolina regains control of the territory

1789—North Carolina gives the Tennessee region to the United States

1790—Congress establishes the Territory of the United States South of the River Ohio, including present-day Tennessee; William Blount becomes the territory's first and only governor; Knoxville is chosen as the seat of territorial government; John Sevier is elected the first representative to the U.S. Congress from west of the Alleghenies

1794—Blount College, the first nonsectarian college in the United States, is chartered

1796—The first state constitution is adopted; on June 1, Tennessee is admitted to the Union as the sixteenth state and the first to emerge from territorial status

1797—Thomas Embree, writing in the Knoxville *Gazette*, urges the organization of an abolitionist society

1811-12—Reelfoot Lake, in northwestern Tennessee, is formed by an earthquake

1814—Coal is first mined in Tennessee, in Roane County

1815—Andrew Jackson, leading the Tennessee volunteers, defeats the British at the Battle of New Orleans

1818—In West Tennessee and western Kentucky, Chickasaw lands east of the Mississippi River are acquired in the Jackson Purchase

1819—John Overton lays out the city of Memphis; Elihu Embree publishes the *Manumission Intelligencer*, the first antislavery paper in the United States, in Jonesborough; Murfreesboro becomes the state capital

1826—Nashville becomes the state capital

1828—Tennessean Andrew Jackson is elected the seventh president of the United States

1837—A uniform system of public schools is established

1838—The Cherokees are moved from Tennessee to Oklahoma, on a forced march known as the Trail of Tears; Chattanooga is founded

1843—Nashville becomes the permanent state capital

1844—Tennessean James K. Polk, the first ''dark horse'' in American politics, is elected eleventh president of the United States

1848—Governor Brown calls for volunteers for the Mexican War; Tennessee's quota is 2,800, but 30,000 respond, confirming the reputation of Tennessee as the Volunteer State

1851—The Nashville and Chattanooga Railroad, the first to operate successfully in the state, begins

1861—The Civil War begins; Tennessee secedes from the Union on June 8

1865—The Civil War ends; President Lincoln is assassinated; the Thirteenth Amendment to the Constitution ends slavery in the United States

1866—Tennessee is the first state to be restored to the Union; Fisk University opens in Nashville

1870—Tennessee's third constitution is adopted, giving all males twenty-one years of age and over the right to vote; Randall Brown is elected a Davidson County commissioner, becoming the first black to hold an elective office in Tennessee

1876—Meharry Medical College for blacks is founded as part of Central Tennessee College

1882—Julia Doak is appointed state superintendent of education, the first woman in the United States to hold such an office

1911—The General Assembly passes a child labor law

1915—The Agricultural and Industrial Normal School for blacks is established

1917—The United States enters World War I

1918—Tennessee Sergeant Alvin C. York is awarded the Medal of Honor for capturing 132 men single-handedly; World War I ends

1919—The state enacts a bill giving women the right to vote

1920—Tennessee is the thirty-sixth and deciding state to ratify the Nineteenth Amendment to the U.S. Constitution, granting suffrage to all women in the nation

1925—The famous Scopes trial, a dispute over the teaching of evolution in public schools, draws nationwide attention to Dayton; Grand Ole Opry, later to be a nationally popular radio show, is broadcast from Nashville

1933—Congress establishes the Tennessee Valley Authority; construction of the Norris Dam on the Tennessee River is begun

1936—Norris Dam is completed and produces its first power

1941—The United States enters World War II

1942—The federal government begins building an atomic energy center at Oak Ridge

1945—World War II ends; a public announcement of the atomic bomb project at Oak Ridge focuses world attention on Tennessee

1949—A new Uranium-235 plant and increased facilities for peacetime atomic research are announced for Oak Ridge

1953—Tennessee voters adopt eight amendments, including abolition of the poll tax, proposed by a constitutional convention

1954—The U.S. Supreme Court rules that segregation in public schools is unconstitutional, in opposition to the Tennessee state constitution that states it is illegal for white and black children to attend integrated schools

1956—Desegregation of state-supported schools begins in Clinton

1968—The Reverend Martin Luther King, Jr., a national civil-rights leader, is assassinated in Memphis

1972—The Opryland USA theme park opens in Nashville and attracts 1,400,000 visitors during its first year

1974—Tennessee is declared a disaster area after a devastating tornado

1975—Floods across the state cause millions of dollars' worth of damage

1982—A world's fair is held in Knoxville

1983—The Nashville Metropolitan Board of Education agrees on a settlement that ends twenty-eight years of courtroom battles over school desegregation

1986—Biochemistry professor Stanley Cohen of Vanderbilt University is awarded the Nobel Prize in medicine

1989—Tennessee celebrates the two-hundredth anniversary of the presidency in the United States by honoring the state's three native sons who became president: Andrew Jackson, James K. Polk, and Andrew Johnson

1990—Senator Howard Baker donates his political papers to the University of Tennessee

1991—Former Tennessee governor Lamar Alexander becomes secretary of education in President George Bush's cabinet

IMPORTANT PEOPLE

Roy Acuff (1903-   ), born near Maynardville; country music star, singer, band leader; member of the Grand Ole Opry since 1938; elected to the Country Music Hall of Fame (1962)

James Agee (1909-1955), born in Knoxville; author and critic; famous works include books such as *Let Us Now Praise Famous Men, The Morning Watch*, and the 1958 Pulitzer Prizewinning *Death in the Family*; and the film script for *African Queen*

Eddy Arnold (1918-   ), born in Hendersonville; singer; known as the Tennessee Ploughboy; one of the most successful singers in Nashville's history; elected to the Country Music Hall of Fame (1966)

Chet Atkins (1924-   ), born in Luttrell; producer and guitarist; one of the creators of the Nashville Sound; named Instrumentalist of the Year eight times

Howard Henry Baker, Jr. (1925-   ), born in Huntsville; lawyer, politician; U.S. senator (1966-87); vice-chairman of the Senate Watergate Committee (1973); Senate majority leader (1981-85); White House chief of staff for President Ronald Reagan (1987-88)

Edward Emerson Barnard (1857-1923), born in Nashville; astronomer; pioneer in celestial photography; discovered Jupiter's fifth moon in 1892; also discovered sixteen comets

Polly Bergen (1930-   ), born in Knoxville; actress, singer, television star, film producer; founder and owner of a cosmetics business

William Blount (1749-1800), the first (and only) governor of the Territory of the United States South of the River Ohio; led Tennessee to statehood; U.S. senator (1796-97)

Arna Wendell Bontemps (1902-1973), writer, librarian; author-in-residence and librarian at Fisk University; wrote more than twenty works on the history, literature, and folklore of blacks

CHET ATKINS

EDWARD E. BARNARD

ARNA BONTEMPS

DOROTHY BROWN

JOSEPH BYRNS

DAVY CROCKETT

DAVID FARRAGUT

Dr. Dorothy Brown (1919-　　), surgeon, educator, legislator; professor of surgery at Meharry Medical College; the first black woman to practice general surgery in the South; chief of surgery at Riverside Hospital (1960-83); the first black woman elected to the Tennessee General Assembly (1966-68)

Joseph Wellington Byrns (1869-1936), born in Cedar Hill; lawyer, politician; Tennessee state legislator and senator; U.S. representative (1909-36); Democratic majority leader (1932-35); Speaker of the House of Representatives (1935-36)

Tracy Caulkins (1963-　　), grew up in Nashville; Olympic gold-medal swimmer; won forty-eight national titles; set sixty-one American and five world records

Robert R. Church (1839-1912), slave, entrepreneur, philanthropist; freed from slavery at the end of the Civil War; became the South's first black millionaire; was the first person to purchase a $1,000 bond to help restore Memphis after the yellow fever epidemic of 1878; helped in the development of Beale Street

David Crockett (1786-1836), born in Limestown; frontiersman, soldier, politician; a military scout in the War of 1812; Tennessee legislator; U.S. representative (1827-31, 1833-35); was killed in the Battle of the Alamo, Texas

Edward Hull Crump (1874-1954), politician; elected mayor of Memphis in 1909 and served four terms; U.S. representative (1931-35); was an important political "boss" in Tennessee until his death

Sam Davis (1842-1863), born near Smyrna; military scout for the Confederate army; captured, sentenced, and hanged by a Union military court because he had information about the Union army

Dorothy Dix (1861-1951), born Elizabeth Meriwether (Gilmer) in Montgomery County; journalist; author of a newspaper syndicated advice column; author of *Dorothy Dix: Her Book* and *How to Win and Hold a Husband*

Wilma Dykeman (1920-　　), writer; author of *Tennessee: A Bicentennial History* and other books and articles about the South and Tennessee; coauthored *Neither Black nor White* with her husband, the late James Stokely

David Glasgow Farragut (1801-1870), born at Campbell's Station, west of Knoxville; seaman, officer; rose through the ranks to become the first admiral of the U.S. Navy; remained loyal to the Union; in the Battle of Mobile Bay, he uttered the famous words: "Damn the torpedoes! Full speed ahead!"

Cornelia Fort (1919-1943), born in Nashville; pilot; first woman pilot to die in the service of her country (World War II)

Morris Frank (1908-1980), born in Nashville; owned the first seeing-eye dog in the United States; leader in the Seeing Eye organization that was founded in Nashville

Albert Gore, Jr. (1948-   ), lawyer, politician; U.S. representative (1976-85); U.S. senator (1985-   )

Alex Palmer Haley (1921-   ), moved to Henning in early childhood; journalist and writer; author of *Roots: The Saga of an American Family*, for which he received a special Pulitzer Prize in 1977

William C. Handy (1873-1958), bandleader, solo cornetist, composer, music publisher; wrote the first blues songs on Beale Street in Memphis; his best-known song is "St. Louis Blues"; others include "Beale Street Blues," "Memphis Blues," "Mississippi Blues," and "Harlem Blues"; author of *W. C. Handy's Collection of Negro Spirituals*

W. C. HANDY

Samuel Houston (1793-1863), soldier and politician; fought in Creek Indian War; U.S. representative (1823-27); governor of Tennessee (1827-29); as commander-in-chief of the Texas army, led his forces to victory in the Texas Revolution (1836); first president of the Republic of Texas (1836-38, 1841-44); U.S. senator from Texas (1846-59); governor of Texas (1859-61)

Cordell Hull (1871-1955), born in Overton; statesman; U.S. representative (1907-21, 1923-31); U.S. senator (1931-33); author of the Income Tax Law (1913) and Federal Inheritance Tax Law (1916); U.S. secretary of state (1933-44); author of the Good Neighbor Policy (1933) among the North and South American nations; cited as Father of the United Nations Organization; awarded Nobel Peace Prize (1945)

ESTES KEFAUVER

Andrew Jackson (1767-1845), seventh president of the United States (1829-37); nicknamed Old Hickory; U.S. representative (1796-97); U.S. senator (1797-98, 1823-25); hero of the Battle of New Orleans (1815); lived in Nashville at The Hermitage

Andrew Johnson (1808-1875), seventeenth president of the United States (1865-69); U.S. representative (1843-53); governor of Tennessee (1853-57); U.S. senator (1857-62); military governor of Tennessee (1862-65); vice-president of U.S. (1865)

Estes Kefauver (1903-1963), born in Madisonville; lawyer, politician; U.S. representative (1939-49); U.S. senator (1949-63); gained nationwide fame as chairman of the Senate crime committee

CAMILLE KELLEY

Camille McGee Kelley (1883?-1955), born in Trenton; the first woman judge in the South (1920-50) and the second in the nation

Joseph Wood Krutch (1893-1970), born in Knoxville; critic, essayist, conservationist, educator; professor of English at Columbia University (1937-52); biographer of Edgar Allan Poe, Samuel Johnson, and Henry Thoreau; drama critic for *The Nation*

Loretta Lynn (1935-   ), songwriter, singer; Grand Old Opry star; the first woman named Entertainer of the Year by the Country Music Association (1972)

JOSEPH KRUTCH

PATRICIA NEAL

ROBERT NEYLAND

SAM RAYBURN

GRANTLAND RICE

Mary Noailles Murfree (1850-1922), born in Murfreesboro; novelist; wrote under the pen name Charles Egbert Craddock; her works include a collection of stories called *In the Tennessee Mountains* and novels *The Juggler, The Windfall,* and *The Ordeal*

Patricia Neal (1926-   ), born in Knoxville; actress; won an Academy Award as best actress for her performance in *Hud* (1963); battled the effects of three massive strokes to return to acting

Robert Reese Neyland, Jr. (1892-1962), soldier, teacher, football coach; brigadier general in the U.S. Army; professor of military tactics and famous head football coach and athletic director at the University of Tennessee

Adolph Simon Ochs (1858-1935), newspaper publisher; educated in Knoxville; owner and publisher of the *Chattanooga Times* (1878-1935); owner and publisher of the *New York Times* (1896-1935)

Dolly Parton (1946-   ), born in Sevierville; singer, songwriter, movie and television star; owner of Dollywood family theme park in Pigeon Forge

Minnie Pearl (1912-   ), born Sarah Ophelia Colley (Cannon) in Centerville; comedienne; star of the Grand Ole Opry; spokesperson and goodwill ambassador for Tennessee; named to Country Music Hall of Fame (1972)

Carl Perkins (1932-   ), born in Jackson; rock and roll singer and songwriter; composed "Blue Suede Shoes"; recorded for original Sun Records in Memphis

James Knox Polk (1795-1849), eleventh president of the United States (1845-49); U.S. representative (1825-39); Speaker of the House (1835-39); governor of Tennessee (1839-41)

Elvis Aron Presley (1935-1977), singer, actor; lived at Graceland, in Memphis; fused rhythm and blues with country and western music styles to become the king of rock and roll; one of the most popular entertainers of the second half of the twentieth century

Sam Rayburn (1882-1961), born in Roane County; U.S. representative from Texas (1913-61); Speaker of the House (1940-46, 1949-53, 1955-61); helped pass many of President Franklin D. Roosevelt's New Deal programs.

Grantland Rice (1880-1954), born in Murfreesboro; sportswriter known as the dean of American sportswriters; wrote for the *New York Herald Tribune*; gave Notre Dame's 1924 football backfield the nickname "The Four Horsemen"

Felix Robertson (1781-1865), born in Nashville; the first white child born in Nashville; became mayor of the city

James Robertson (1742-1814), pioneer Indian fighter; brought the first settlers to the present-day site of Nashville; is called the Father of Tennessee

John Ross (1790-1866), born near Lookout Mountain; Indian leader; president of the National Council of Cherokees (1819-26); chief of the United Cherokee Nation (1828-39); united the eastern and western branches of the Cherokees; resisted the removal of the Cherokees, but led the nation to Oklahoma

Carl Thomas Rowan (1925-), born near Ravenscroft; journalist, diplomat; ambassador to Finland (1963); director of the U.S. Information Service (1964); writer of a syndicated newspaper column

JOHN ROSS

Wilma Rudolph (1940-), born in Clarksville; athlete; overcame partial invalidism as a child to set the world's record for the woman's 100-meter dash (1961); won three gold medals in the 1960 Olympic Games

Clarence Saunders (1881-1953), born in Memphis; entrepreneur; originated the self-service market and founded the Piggly Wiggly supermarket chain

Dr. Margaret Rhea Seddon (1947-), born in Murfreesboro; physician, astronaut; made a historic seven-day flight aboard the space shuttle *Discovery*, April 12-19, 1985

Sequoyah (1760?-1843), born in Monroe County; silversmith, painter, warrior, scholar; invented the Cherokee alphabet of eighty-six characters; taught many of his people to read and write

CARL ROWAN

John Sevier (1745-1815), soldier, politician; led Tennessee in the Battle of Kings Mountain (1780); governor of the short-lived state of Franklin (1785-88); U.S. representative (1789-91, 1811-15); the first governor of Tennessee (1796-1801, 1803-09)

Cybill Shepherd (1950-), born in Memphis; actress, singer, model, television star; best known for her work in the movie *The Last Picture Show* and in the television series "Moonlighting"

Dinah Shore (1917-), born in Winchester; singer, actress, television personality, sports enthusiast

Bessie Smith (1894-1937), born in Chattanooga; singer, songwriter; considered one of the greatest blues singers in history

CLARENCE SAUNDERS

Frederick Wallace Smith (1944-), pilot, entrepreneur; founded the Federal Express Corporation, based in Memphis

Nancy Ward (1738-1824), born in the Cherokee village Chota; Indian leader; known as Prophetess and Beloved Woman of the Cherokee Nation; warned settlers of impending attacks by pro-British Cherokees (1776, 1780); credited with teaching Indian women the art of raising cattle and of making butter and cheese

Ida B. Wells (1862-1931), journalist, publisher; owned and edited the *Memphis Free Press*; fought racial discrimination and disenfranchisement based on race or sex; well known for her articulate reporting on the horrors of lynching; founded the Negro Fellowship League (1910)

JOHN SEVIER

ALVIN YORK

Oprah Winfrey (1954-   ), talk show host, actress, entrepreneur; graduated from Tennessee State University, Nashville; host of a nationally syndicated television talk show; owns a television production company (Harpo)

Alvin C. York (1887-1964), born near Pall Mall; soldier, humanitarian; became the greatest American hero of World War I and one of the most effective combat soldiers in American history; awarded the Congressional Medal of Honor, the French Croix de Guerre with palms, and the Tennessee Medal for Valor; after the war, he gave lectures to raise money for the industrial school now known as Alvin York Institute and for a Bible school

GOVERNORS

John Sevier	1796-1801	Robert Love Taylor	1897-1899
Archibald Roane	1801-1803	Benton McMillin	1899-1903
John Sevier	1803-1809	James B. Frazier	1903-1905
Willie Blount	1809-1815	John I. Cox	1905-1907
Joseph McMinn	1815-1821	Malcolm R. Patterson	1907-1911
William Carroll	1821-1827	Ben W. Hooper	1911-1915
Sam Houston	1827-1829	Tom C. Rye	1915-1919
William Hall	1829	A. H. Roberts	1919-1921
William Carroll	1829-1835	Alfred A. Taylor	1921-1923
Newton Cannon	1835-1839	Austin Peay	1923-1927
James K. Polk	1839-1841	Henry H. Horton	1927-1933
James C. Jones	1841-1845	Hill McAlister	1933-1937
Aaron V. Brown	1845-1847	Gordon Browning	1937-1939
Neill S. Brown	1847-1849	Prentice Cooper	1939-1945
William Trousdale	1849-1851	Jim McCord	1945-1949
William B. Campbell	1851-1853	Gordon Browning	1949-1953
Andrew Johnson	1853-1857	Frank G. Clement	1953-1959
Isham G. Harris	1857-1862	Buford Ellington	1959-1963
Andrew Johnson	1862-1865	Frank G. Clement	1963-1967
William G. Brownlow	1865-1869	Buford Ellington	1967-1971
DeWitt Clinton Senter	1869-1871	Winfield Dunn	1971-1975
John C. Brown	1871-1875	Leonard Ray Blanton	1975-1979
James D. Porter	1875-1879	Lamar Alexander	1979-1987
Albert S. Marks	1879-1881	Ned Ray McWherter	1987-
Alvin Hawkins	1881-1883		
William B. Bate	1883-1887		
Robert Love Taylor	1887-1891		
John P. Buchanan	1891-1893		
Peter Turney	1893-1897		

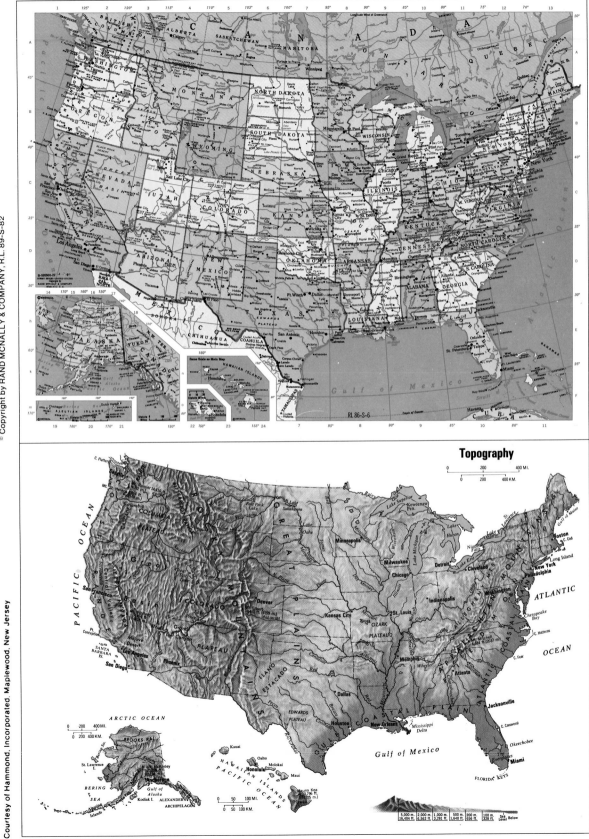

Topography

0   200   400 MI.

0   200   400 KM.

MAP KEY

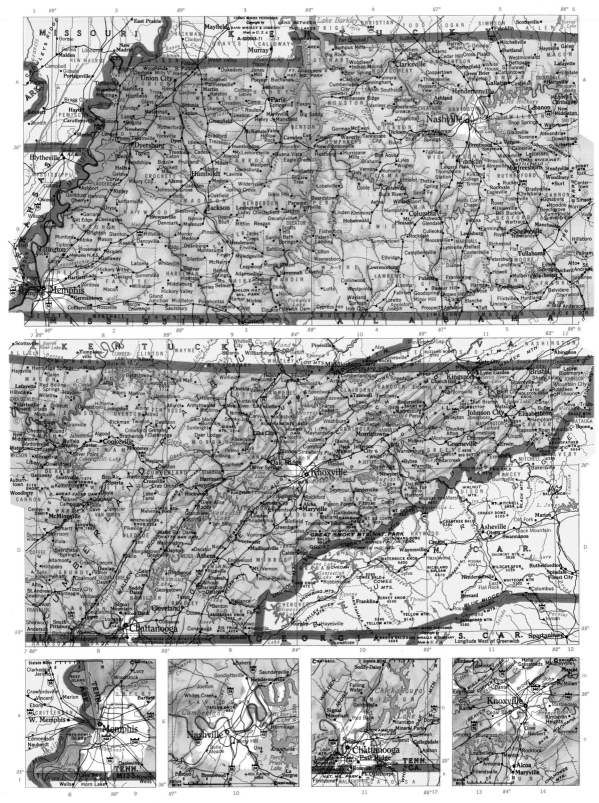

Lambert Conformal Conic Projection

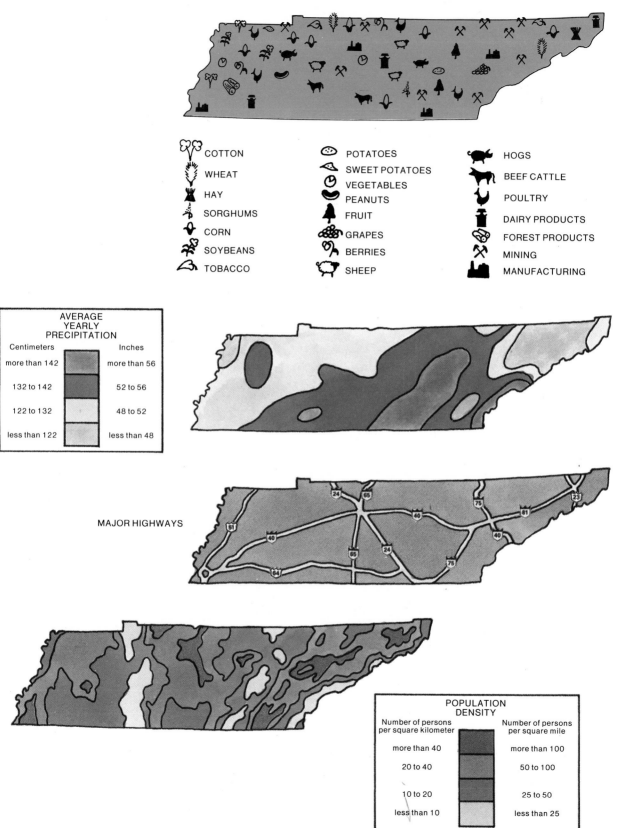

COTTON
WHEAT
HAY
SORGHUMS
CORN
SOYBEANS
TOBACCO

POTATOES
SWEET POTATOES
VEGETABLES
PEANUTS
FRUIT
GRAPES
BERRIES
SHEEP

HOGS
BEEF CATTLE
POULTRY
DAIRY PRODUCTS
FOREST PRODUCTS
MINING
MANUFACTURING

AVERAGE
YEARLY
PRECIPITATION

Centimeters		Inches
more than 142		more than 56
132 to 142		52 to 56
122 to 132		48 to 52
less than 122		less than 48

MAJOR HIGHWAYS

POPULATION
DENSITY

Number of persons per square kilometer		Number of persons per square mile
more than 40		more than 100
20 to 40		50 to 100
10 to 20		25 to 50
less than 10		less than 25

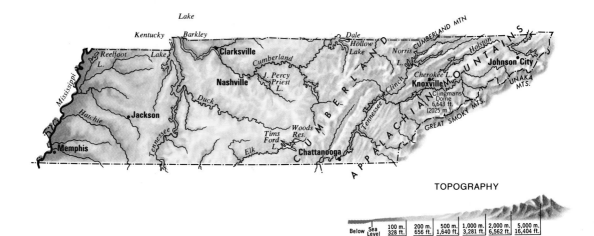

Lake Kentucky Lake Barkley

Reelfoot L.

Mississippi

Hatchie

Memphis

Jackson

Tennessee

Duck

Cumberland

Clarksville

Nashville

J. Percy Priest L.

Tims Ford L.

Woods Res.

Elk

Chattanooga

Dale Hollow Lake

CUMBERLAND MTN

Norris L.

CUMBERLAND

Clinch

Tennessee

Cherokee L.

Knoxville

Clingmans Dome 6,643 ft. (2025 m.)

GREAT SMOKY MTS.

Holston

Johnson City

APPALACHIAN MOUNTAINS

UNAKA MTS.

TOPOGRAPHY

Below Sea Level	100 m. 328 ft.	200 m. 656 ft.	500 m. 1,640 ft.	1,000 m. 3,281 ft.	2,000 m. 6,562 ft.	5,000 m. 16,404 ft.

Courtesy of Hammond, Incorporated
Maplewood, New Jersey

COUNTIES

Tiptonville LAKE

OBION Union City WEAKLEY HENRY
Dresden Paris

DYER Dyersburg GIBSON Trenton Camden STEWART Clarksville Dover ROBERTSON Springfield SUMNER Gallatin Lafayette MACON CLAY Celina PICKETT Byrdstown Jamestown SCOTT Huntsville CAMPBELL Jacksboro CLAIBORNE Tazewell UNION Maynardville Sneedville HANCOCK HAWKINS Rogersville Blountville SULLIVAN Mountain City JOHNSON

LAUDERDALE Ripley CROCKETT Alamo Huntingdon CARROLL BENTON Waverly HOUSTON Erin MONTGOMERY Charlotte DICKSON Ashland City CHEATHAM DAVIDSON NASHVILLE Lebanon WILSON Carthage SMITH Gainesboro JACKSON Livingston OVERTON FENTRESS Cookeville PUTNAM Wartburg MORGAN Clinton ANDERSON Knoxville KNOX Dandridge JEFFERSON Morristown HAMBLEN Newport COCKE GREENE Greeneville WASHINGTON Jonesboro Elizabethton CARTER UNICOI

HAYWOOD Brownsville Jackson MADISON HENDERSON Lexington DECATUR Decaturville PERRY Linden Centerville HICKMAN Franklin WILLIAMSON Columbia MAURY RUTHERFORD Murfreesboro Woodbury CANNON DE KALB Smithville Sparta WHITE Crossville CUMBERLAND ROANE Kingston Loudon LOUDON Maryville BLOUNT Sevierville SEVIER

TIPTON Covington Brownsville CHESTER Henderson Savannah Waynesboro LAWRENCE Lawrenceburg LEWIS Hohenwald MARSHALL Lewisburg BEDFORD Shelbyville Manchester COFFEE WARREN McMinnville GRUNDY Altamont Spencer VAN BUREN BLEDSOE Pikeville Dayton RHEA Decatur MEIGS Madisonville MONROE

SHELBY Memphis FAYETTE Somerville HARDEMAN Bolivar MC NAIRY Selmer HARDIN WAYNE GILES Pulaski LINCOLN Fayetteville FRANKLIN Winchester Lynchburg MOORE MARION Jasper Chattanooga HAMILTON Cleveland BRADLEY Benton POLK

Autumn colors in the foothills of the Smoky Mountains near Gatlinburg

INDEX

Page numbers that appear in boldface type indicate illustrations

Knoxville firemen in front of their fire truck

Picture Identifications

Front Cover: Miller Homestead, Roan Mountain State Resort Park
Back Cover: Great Smoky Mountains National Park
Pages 2-3: Sunset in the Great Smoky Mountains
Page 6: A statue of W. C. Handy on Beale Street, Memphis
Pages 8-9: Roaring Fork, Great Smoky Mountains National Park
Pages 20-21: Montage of Tennesseans
Page 26: Rocky Mount, the first capitol of the Territory of the United States South of the River Ohio
Pages 38-39: A woman spinning at Homeplace 1850, a living-history farm at Land Between the Lakes
Page 52: Norris Dam and lake
Pages 62-63: The state capitol (on the right) at Legislative Plaza, Nashville
Pages 72-73: Center Stage, the new Roy Acuff theater at Opryland USA
Pages 86-87: Azaleas blooming on the grounds of a fieldstone house in Knoxville during the April Dogwood Festival
Page 108: Montage showing the state flag, the state tree (tulip tree), the state wild animal (raccoon), the state cultivated flower (iris), and the state bird (mockingbird)

About the Author

Sylvia McNair is the author of numerous books for adults and young people about interesting places. A graduate of Oberlin College, she has toured all fifty of the United States and more than thirty foreign countries. Her travels have included many visits to all sections of Tennessee. Always interested in education, she served for six years on a district school board in Illinois. McNair now lives in Evanston, Illinois. She has three sons, one daughter, and two grandsons.

Picture Acknowledgments

Front cover: © H. Abernathy/**H. Armstrong Roberts**; 2-3, © D. & I. MacDonald/**Photri**; 4, © Bob Glander/**Shostal/SuperStock**; 5, **The Peabody Hotel, Memphis**; 6, © Matthew Kaplan/**Marilyn Gartman Agency**; 8-9, © **Mack & Betty Kelley**; 11, © **John Netherton**; 13, © Wilson Goodrich/**Marilyn Gartman Agency**; 14, © **Tom Raymond**; 15, © Ken Dequaine Photography/**Third Coast Stock Source**; 17, © T. Algire/**H. Armstrong Roberts**; 19 (left), © **John Netherton**; 19 (right), © **Mack & Betty Kelley**; 20 (top left, bottom left), © **Joan Dunlop**; 20 (middle left, top right), © **Tom Raymond**; 20 (bottom right), © **Jeff Greenberg**; 21 (top left), © Bill Barksdale/**Root Resources**; 21 (bottom left, middle), © **Joan Dunlop**; 21 (middle right, middle bottom), © **Tom Raymond**; 21 (bottom right), © **Jeff Greenberg**; 23, © **Jeff Greenberg**; 24, © **Tom Raymond**; 26, © H. Abernathy/**H. Armstrong Roberts**; 30 (left), **Historical Pictures Service, Chicago**; 30 (right), © **Jeff Greenberg**; 33, **Historical Pictures Service, Chicago**; 34 (left), © **Matt Bradley**; 34 (right), **Library of Congress**; 37, **San Jacinto Museum of History Association**; 38-39, © **Arch McLean**; 41 (left), **Historical Pictures Service, Chicago**; 41 (right), **North Wind Picture Archives**; 42 (left), **Library of Congress**; 42 (right), **Historical Pictures Service, Chicago**; 45, **Historical Pictures Service, Chicago**; 47, **Library of Congress**; 48 (both pictures), © **Tom Raymond**; 50, **Historical Pictures Service, Chicago**; 52, © **Mack & Betty Kelley**; 55, **UPI/Bettmann Newsphotos**; 58, **AP/Wide World Photos**; 61, © **Cameramann International, Ltd.**; 62-63, © R. Krubner/**H. Armstrong Roberts**; 65, © **Joan Dunlop**; 66 (left), © **Jeff Greenberg**; 66 (right), © Linda Lottmann/**Photo Options**; 68, © D. Donne Bryant/**Root Resources**; 69 (left), © J. C. Allen & Son, Inc./**Root Resources**; 69 (right), © Helen Kittinger/**Photo Options**; 70, © **Cameramann, International, Ltd.**; 71, © Robin Smith/**Shostal/SuperStock**; 72-73, © **Matt Bradley**; 75, **Wide World Photos, Inc.**; 78, © **Mack & Betty Kelley**; 79, © **Matt Bradley**; 80 (left), **Wide World Photos, Inc.**; 80 (right), © **Donnie Beauchamp/Opryland USA**; 81, © **Donnie Beauchamp/Opryland USA**; 83 (left), © **Martin Hintz**; 83 (right), **AP/Wide World Photos**; 84, **North Wind Picture Archives**; 85, © Nancy Boyd Johnson/**Photo Options**; 86-87, © Ken Dequaine, Photographer/**Third Coast Stock Source**; 89, © **H. Armstrong Roberts**; 90 (both pictures), © **Mack & Betty Kelley**; 91 (left), © **Jeff Greenberg**; 91 (map), **Len Meents**; 92, © Scott Berner/**Photri**; 95 (left), © **Matt Bradley**; 95 (map), **Len Meents**; 96 (left), © F. Sieb/**H. Armstrong Roberts**; 96 (right), © D. & I. MacDonald/**Root Resources**; 97, © **Tom Raymond**; 98, © H. Abernathy/**H. Armstrong Roberts**; 100, © D. Muench/**H. Armstrong Roberts**; 101 (left), © **Matt Bradley**; 101 (map), **Len Meents**; 102 (left), © **Matt Bradley**; 102 (right), **Shostal/SuperStock**; 104, © **Mack & Betty Kelley**; 105, © R. Krubner/**H. Armstrong Roberts**; 107 (right), © R. Krubner/**H. Armstrong Roberts**; 107 (left), © **Joan Dunlop**; 108 (background), © Kitty Kohout/**Root Resources**; 108 (raccoon), © E. R. Degginger/**H. Armstrong Roberts**; 108 (flag), **Courtesy Flag Research Center, Winchester, Massachusetts 01890**; 108 (iris), © Louise K. Broman/**Root Resources**; 108 (mockingbird), **Shostal/SuperStock**; 114, © Chuck Snow Photo Inc./**Photo Options**; 119, © **Tom Raymond**; 121, © H. Abernathy/**H. Armstrong Roberts**; 122, © **Martin Hintz**; 127 (top and bottom), **AP/Wide World Photos**; 127 (middle), **North Wind Picture Archives**; 128 (Brown, Byrns, and Farragut), **AP/Wide World Photos**; 128 (Crockett), **Historical Pictures Service, Chicago**; 129 (Handy, Kelley, and Krutch), **AP/Wide World Photos**; 129 (Kefauver), **Historical Pictures Service, Chicago**; 130 (Neal, Neyland, and Rice), **AP/Wide World Photos**; 130 (Rayburn), **Historical Pictures Service, Chicago**; 131 (Ross, Rowan, and Saunders), **Historical Pictures Service, Chicago**; 131 (Sevier), **North Wind Picture Archives**; 132, **AP/Wide World Photos**; 138, © Ken Dequaine Photography/**Third Coast Stock Source**; 141, © **Matt Bradley**; back cover, © Bob Brudd/**TSW-Click/Chicago Ltd.**